The Right One

MarriageToday™
P.O. Box 59888
Dallas, Texas 75229

1-800-380-6330

www.marriagetoday.com

ISBN 978-0-9914820-7-8

Printed in the United States of America

FOREWORD

by Kari Jobe

When Jimmy Evans asked me to write the foreword for his newest book, I was not only honored, but eager to help out.

I'm honored because I have so much respect for Pastor Jimmy and his teachings. I've been privileged over the last ten years to serve under his leadership at Gateway Church in Southlake, Texas, and have seen firsthand his father's heart and pastor's spirit. He is a leader of leaders, and a blessing to the body of Christ, and I couldn't be more honored by his request.

I'm also thrilled to help out because I believe so strongly in the message of this book. Being a Christian single in today's culture can be a long and confusing journey, and one that each of us has to navigate on our walk of faith. Finding the right marriage partner is a difficult endeavor, and one of the most critical decisions many of us will ever face. The solid, no-nonsense advice that Jimmy and Frank relay in this book is not only welcome, but greatly needed.

For me, the timing of this book couldn't be more appropriate. Less than two weeks ago, I became engaged to the man of my dreams—to my best friend and fellow worship leader, Cody Carnes! Those who know Cody can attest to his tremendous faith and godly character. I can't wait to become his life partner and soul mate! He is truly the man of God that I've been searching for, and I thank the Lord for bringing us together.

My journey toward finding The Right One was not an easy one. Before I found my husband, I dated good Christian men, but none ever felt quite right for me. Some years ago, I began dating a man that I was sure God wanted me to marry someday. On paper we seemed perfect for each other. We were both worship leaders, both pursuing a career in music, and both in love with Jesus. We had almost all of the same friends, and many common interests and dreams.

"ALWAYS REMEMBER; IF YOU DON'T HAVE THE PEACE OF THE HOLY SPIRIT, THEY ARE NOT THE RIGHT ONE FOR YOU"

He was charismatic and a gifted musician, and I quickly fell in love with him. Though in many ways, I think I was more in love with the idea of being his wife, and doing ministry alongside him. In spite of my strong feelings for him, something in my spirit never quite felt at peace about our relationship. We loved each other deeply, but the more time we spent together, the more it became clear that our futures were not aligning.

I've always known that God had a very specific calling on my life and ministry, and that calling was simply not in sync with the calling that he had on his life. We were headed in different directions, and the longer we dated, the more we realized that we were not meant to be together. So after nearly six years of dating, we decided to go our separate ways. I was thirty-one when we broke off the relationship, and it was probably the hardest thing God has ever asked me to do. But I knew I needed to be obedient. He knew it as well. So we parted as friends.

It was just a few months after that breakup that Cody began pursuing my heart, and my first reaction was to resist. He was a good friend, and I didn't want to jeopardize that friendship. So I kept him at arm's length. My friends and family wondered why I was so hesitant, and my pastors would often say to me, "Do you know what an amazing man he is? You two would be so good together!" Yet still I didn't see it.

One day the Lord spoke to my spirit and told me to give Cody a chance, and so I did. Today I look back on that time and find it stunning that it took me so long to see what everyone else seemed to instinctively understand. The Lord opened my eyes and my heart, and today I couldn't be happier. I am engaged to the most wonderful man I've ever met, and I know that God has brought us together for a reason. My spirit is filled with joy and excitement for our future together! We not only love each other deeply, but we have a clear and shared vision for our lives and ministry. We are truly meant to be together!

If there is one message I'd like to relay to those who are still searching for a spouse, it would be this: don't allow yourself to get so caught up in the idea of marriage that you miss the voice of the Holy Spirit. That's not fair to you, and it's not fair to the people you date. When you fall in love with someone, make sure you love them for who they are, not what you long for them to be. And always remember; if you don't have the peace of the Holy Spirit, they are not the right one for you.

My prayer is that every single person would find the kind of blessed and fulfilling relationship that Cody and I have discovered. I long for every young woman to find a man as loving and devoted and perfect for her as Cody is for me. And for every young man to become such a person in order to attract the woman of his dreams.

Jimmy Evans and Frank Martin have that same longing, and they've created one of the best resources I've seen on finding and marrying the right person. Whether you are engaged to be married, in a serious dating relationship, or still single and looking for the right life partner, you will find timeless and biblical advice on the pages that follow.

The Right One is truly a godsend for those of us who need clear guidance and direction when seeking the person God has for our future.

When you are single, it is so easy to invest your heart and life in the wrong person. I know that truth firsthand. But don't allow yourself to fall into that trap. When God's best is waiting for you right around the corner, it is a spiritual and emotional tragedy to settle for anything less.

I've learned through this season that it's so important to trust the Lord. He wants the best for each one of us, so trust him, and obey his voice quickly. If you do, he will guide you and help you find The Right One for you. It's a journey of faith for sure, and well worth it.

Regardless of where you are on your journey toward marriage, I encourage you to read this book slowly and deliberately, and even re-read those sections that speak most clearly to your spirit. Allow God to mentor you through these pages, and guide you as you seek his will for your future. I've been so blessed by Jimmy and Frank's godly wisdom and advice, and I promise you will be blessed as well.

Kari Jobe
Southlake, Texas

The Right One

How to Successfully Date and Marry the Right Person

JIMMY EVANS & FRANK MARTIN

BEFORE
YOU
BEGIN

There are a few things you should know before you begin.

First, even though this book is a collaboration between two authors, we decided to write in the "voice" of one—in the singular first person tense. Constantly writing "we think this," or "we believe that," can quickly feel cumbersome and confusing, so instead we've defaulted to the singular "I." The only exceptions are those times when a personal story or example is told. In those cases we've identified who is speaking in parentheses.

Second, in order to preserve the confidences of friends and clients, we've taken the liberty of changing names and identifying facts whenever necessary. The stories we tell are true, but many of the identities have been purposely shielded. So if you think you recognize someone from one of our examples, you're probably wrong. We hope this approach makes for engaging reading, while still retaining credibility with those who come to us for counsel and advice.

Finally, and most importantly, though much of this book is intended as a guide for dating couples to assess the strength of their relationship, it should not be seen as a substitute for pre-marital counseling. We encourage you to use it as a precursor to counseling, perhaps even an additional resource, but not as an alternative. In our opinion, pre-marital counseling is a must for any couple considering marriage, no matter how confident and well prepared they feel.

The Proverbs writer tells us, "The way of fools seems right to them, but the wise listen to counsel." When it comes to making one of the biggest decisions of your life, you need all the advice and counsel you can get. And what better place to look than a pastor, church leader, or Christian counselor?

--Jimmy and Frank

CHAPTER ONE

TILL DEATH DO US PART

Chelsea first met Jim at a Bible study for young adults. He was new in town and looking for a church home. She remembers well their first conversation.

"He came over to where I was sitting and introduced himself, and I thought I was going to pass out!" she says, laughing. "He was so handsome and charming! I could hardly breathe!"

Apparently the attraction was mutual, because the very next week he asked if she'd like to meet him for coffee. It was their first real date, and the beginning of a whirlwind romance. Within a few short weeks they had become an item, and before long they were inseparable. Mutual friends say they can't remember ever seeing Jim and Chelsea when they weren't together.

By all appearances they seemed to be the perfect couple. They both loved hiking and backpacking and going to baseball games. They liked the same movies and even shared the same taste in music. They could often be found sitting side by side in the corner of their favorite coffee shop, sharing a latte, with both headsets plugged into the same iPod.

They were also heavily involved in their church's college ministry. Jim became a small group leader and often helped teach classes. And Chelsea played keyboards on the worship team. They were an integral part of the ministry, and on track to become team leaders.

Exactly one year into their courtship, Jim popped the question. No one was surprised since their friends all assumed they'd be getting married one day. Their relationship seemed like a storybook romance—two "soul mates" who found each other, quickly fell in love, and now were on their way to living happily ever after. On the surface, everything about their relationship appeared perfect.

But appearances can often be deceiving. Though Jim and Chelsea seemed completely happy and content, deep down, Chelsea was having serious doubts. She never talked about it to family or friends, but somehow things between them didn't feel quite right.

Warning Signs

Jim was a personable guy with lots of great qualities, but he had a problem with anger. Chelsea wanted to believe that it was a small problem, just a habit of losing his temper from time to time when things didn't go his way. But soon Jim's fits of anger became more frequent.

Once at a restaurant, a waiter accidentally dropped a glass of tea next to their table, and it splashed on Jim's shoes and pants leg. He snapped at the waiter, calling him a "clumsy idiot," and demanded to see the manager. Though the staff apologized, Jim wouldn't let the matter go. Chelsea was horrified and embarrassed, and the two didn't speak for the rest of the evening.

"APPEARANCES CAN OFTEN BE DECEIVING. "

It was usually a minor annoyance that set Jim off. Like someone cutting him off on the highway, or a cashier at the grocery store who moved too slowly when he was in a hurry. Chelsea was convinced that Jim had a good heart, so she always forgave him for his outbursts. She knew he was under a lot of stress at work and school, and thought that maybe his quick temper was just a phase he was going through. And his fits of anger were seldom aimed at her, so she had no reason to fear him.

At least not until they had their first real argument.

It happened about six months into their courtship. Jim and Chelsea had been invited to a mutual friend's wedding and Chelsea was running behind schedule.

She scrambled to get ready while Jim waited in the front room of her apartment. She could tell he was getting impatient by the tone of his voice.

"How much longer?" he would ask, over and over. "We're going to be late!"

Chelsea was hurrying as fast as she could, but it wasn't fast enough. Suddenly, in a fit of rage, Jim screamed at the top of his lungs, "What are you doing in there? We have to leave now!"

Chelsea quickly grabbed her purse and ran to the front room, even though she wasn't quite finished getting ready. Jim stood with his jaw clenched tightly. "It's about time!" he said angrily, storming out the front door.

It was the first time she'd found herself on the business end of his rage, but not the last. As the relationship grew, his angry outbursts got worse. It wasn't long before he was calling her names and abusing her verbally, though never in public.

Chelsea was deeply concerned about Jim's behavior, but she didn't want to give up on the relationship. In so many ways he seemed like a kind and thoughtful person, and he always apologized after losing his temper. He also seemed sincere about his Christian faith. She wanted to believe that he could change. He was her best friend, and lots of fun to be around. He just had this one problem he couldn't seem to overcome. And down deep, Chelsea hoped that she could be the one to help him overcome it.

Dodging a Bullet

Thankfully, Chelsea's parents sensed that something wasn't quite right about their relationship, and they insisted that Jim and Chelsea enroll in pre-marital counseling. It only took the counselor two weeks to uncover Jim's unhealthy problem with anger. He confronted Jim about it during their third meeting. After that, Jim refused to go back.

At the advice of the counselor, and the pleading of her parents, Chelsea broke off the engagement. It was the hardest thing she had ever done. But she knew in her heart that staying with Jim would be a terrible mistake.

"I know how much you care for Jim," the counselor told her, "but he is an emotional bully. And emotional abuse can easily lead to physical abuse. Unless he is willing to face his problem and get help, you have almost no hope of building a happy and successful marriage."

Chelsea was fortunate enough to have people in her life who were willing to intervene and steer her away from trouble when they saw it coming. Because of it, she was able to recognize the dangerous red flags in their relationship before it was too late. And Chelsea was wise enough to listen. Not everyone is so fortunate.

Eyes Wide Open

Let's be honest. Most couples on the brink of marriage are more interested in planning a beautiful wedding than honestly assessing their relationship. Couples in love are seldom interested in hearing the candid truth about themselves and their partner. Often, they've invested so much time and effort in finding and impressing their "soul mate" that they can't imagine the future being anything but bright and blissful. They want to believe the best about each other, so that's exactly what they do. They put on blinders and charge forward.

That's why it is so easy for dating couples to overlook dangerous red flags— warning signs that in any other situation would be glaringly obvious. They want the relationship to work, so they look the other way. In many cases they see these red flag warnings but choose to ignore them, hoping they will somehow work themselves out. Of course that seldom happens. Once the wedding bells have faded, seemingly minor problems and character flaws become major sources of conflict.

This book is for those who are intent on avoiding those dangerous pitfalls that catch so many hopeful couples off guard. It's for people who love being in love, but are committed to going into marriage with their eyes wide open. It's for couples who are contemplating marriage and excited about their future lives together, but care enough about each other to make their relationship the best that it can possibly be.

This book is also for those who are still looking for love. For those who have yet to find The Right One, but are intent on not wasting time on the wrong one. For those who understand that marriage is a sacred bond and a lifetime commitment, and should never be entered into lightly.

Jimmy's Story

I (Jimmy) have been teaching and counseling on marriage dynamics for over thirty years. I've counseled thousands of couples through the years in all phases of their relationship, from freshly engaged, to newlyweds, to couples who have been married thirty or forty years. In all that time, I've yet to see a relationship as strained and dysfunctional as Karen and I had during our first few years of marriage.

We were barely nineteen when we got married, and may very well have been the least-prepared couple to ever exchange wedding rings. Our dating relationship was riddled with dangerous red flags, yet we were too young and naïve to recognize them. Because of it, our first years of marriage were like a bad nightmare. We fought so much, and so often, that we soon forgot what it was like to go to bed without being angry.

It was an exhausting experience, and very nearly destroyed our relationship. But God stepped in and miraculously saved our marriage. At a time when neither of us held out a shred of hope, God brought healing and restoration. Because of it, Karen and I have dedicated our lives to helping couples grow strong and healthy marriages.

Today we are happier than we ever imagined possible. With God's help, we've been able to overcome our struggles and build a life together that is as strong and healthy as it is rewarding. And we spend our time teaching other couples to do the same in their own relationships.

God brought us back from the brink of destruction, and now he uses our story to help other couples avoid the many mistakes that we made.

> "FINDING THE RIGHT MARRIAGE PARTNER IS THE SECOND MOST IMPORTANT DECISION ANY OF US WILL EVER MAKE, TRUMPED ONLY BY OUR DECISION TO BECOME FOLLOWERS OF JESUS."

Frank's Story

I (Frank) was twenty-seven and Ruthie was twenty-nine when we exchanged vows, and you would have thought we were old enough to know what we were getting into. But in hindsight, we were profoundly immature. I'm still not sure how we got to the altar so dreadfully unqualified to build a life together.

I say "we," but in truth, I was the real source of the problem. I was self-centered and insecure, with expectations that were patently unrealistic. I expected perfection from Ruthie, yet almost nothing from myself.

We had our first real argument just two days into the honeymoon, and I guess we never settled it, because three years later we were still arguing. We decided to start a family, hoping our struggles would work themselves out, but that only added to the stress.

I'm convinced that the only reason we stayed together is that we were both too stubborn to admit failure. Plus we had both been raised in strong Christian homes, and Christians aren't even supposed to think about the "D" word. We were miserable, but committed to staying married.

Through a series of divine and fortunate events, God began teaching us how to rebuild the love and friendship we once had. We began learning how to embrace our differences instead of fighting against them. I learned how to set healthy and realistic expectations for marriage—not to lower them, but to instead focus them on myself instead of Ruthie. And Ruthie learned how to live with an obstinate man and still be in love.

This year we celebrated twenty-eight years of marriage, and we've never been happier. Today our children are in their early twenties. Our daughter is just a few months away from getting married to a wonderful young man, and our son is single, still looking for the right marriage partner. Our primary goal at the moment is to keep them from making the same dreaded mistakes that we made at their stage in life.

The Right One

Finding the right marriage partner is the second most important decision any of us will ever make, trumped only by our decision to become followers of Jesus. It's a decision that affects every aspect of life, and has a profound impact on our future happiness—not only our future, but our children's, and their children, and every generation to come. If there's one decision in life you want to get right, it's this one.

This book is an unapologetic attempt to give you all the tools and information you need to do just that.

We'll begin with some frank and honest talk for dating couples. We'll expose some of the myths of love that people buy into, and why our unrealistic expectations create so many problems in marriages. We'll also discuss the right and wrong ways to date in order to have the best chance for a successful marriage.

Next we'll take an in-depth look at what it takes to grow a strong and healthy marriage. We'll see why some couples succeed while so many others fail. And we'll give insight into how you can head off problems before they even have a chance to begin.

Finally we'll discuss some of the more specific issues that married couples have to deal with on a daily basis. This third section is intended to give you and your potential partner some talking points—some rubber-meets-the-road questions to explore together, just to make sure you're both going into marriage with your eyes wide open.

When it comes to finding the right marriage partner, it's impossible to overthink your future. So stay with me as we explore this important journey together.

SECTION ONE

Straight Talk About
Healthy Dating

CHAPTER TWO

THE MYTHS OF LOVE

A researcher once posed the question, "What makes a good marriage?"

Ninety percent of those who responded answered, "Being in love." These results aren't surprising, but they are telling. When it comes to love and marriage, most of us are pretty idealistic. We want to believe that love is the answer to every problem we have. Years ago the Beatles told us "love is all you need," and we've believed them ever since.

But if "being in love" were all that was needed to grow a happy marriage, the divorce rate would be non-existent.

"Love" is perhaps the most misunderstood and overused word in the English language. A young man will say, "I love my girlfriend," and in the very next breath say, "I love my Dodge truck." A woman will say, "I love my husband," then with the same zeal proclaim to "love" going to Costa Rica, or watching old movies, or getting a pedicure. Even our language betrays how little we understand about the true nature and meaning of love. As well as what it takes to grow a strong and happy love relationship.

When Love Fails

Each year, more than two million couples in the United States stand at the altar and recite their wedding vows. That's more than four million men and women, each filled with hope and optimism, standing before God and their friends, pledging to stay together through thick and thin, through good and bad times, until death parts them. I'm certain that each and every one of those couples are intent on staying true to their vows. Yet if statistics hold true, many of those marriages will eventually end in divorce—most before the seventh year of marriage.

The sad thing is, it doesn't have to be that way. Most failed marriages could be prevented with the right marital advice and counseling. At the very least, many of those headed for trouble could be taught to recognize dangerous red flags before it is too late.

At its core, divorce is nothing more than the result of two people lacking the skills and preparation to navigate the inevitable storms of marriage. It can almost always be avoided with the right counsel and training.

Relationships don't end because couples are not sincere. They end because couples are not equipped to make the marriage last.

And the time to head off relational problems is before they begin. Before the damage has already been done. Before the dysfunction in the relationship has created untold pain and heartache within the marriage.

The time to heal—or avoid—a dysfunctional relationship is long before it turns into a binding marital covenant.

Buying Into The Myths of Love

As I (Frank) look back on the early years of my marriage, I have a number of profound regrets. And most of those regrets revolve around my unrealistic expectations of marriage.

I've always been something of a hopeless romantic. Even as a young man I enjoyed watching sappy romance movies, like "Sleepless in Seattle," and "When Harry Met Sally." When hanging out with buddies, it was all about James Bond and Rambo—the more guns and car chases the better. But another side of me also enjoyed more thoughtful and sensitive films. I think I enjoyed "chick flicks" almost as much as my dates did.

Because of that, I believe I developed a distorted and unhealthy view of romance at an early age. It's not that I didn't understand the importance of commitment and hard work in marriage; I just had a romanticized view of relationships. Like a lot of young, single people, I had bought into many of the damaging myths of love perpetuated by Hollywood.

> "IT'S SO EASY TO BELIEVE THAT LOVE SHOULD LOOK AND FEEL LIKE IT DOES ON THE BIG SCREEN."

Perhaps the most prevalent of these myths is that love is a feeling. And if you don't feel in love, you're with the wrong person.

Myth #1: Love is a Feeling

It's so easy to believe that love should look and feel like it does on the big screen. That once we find and capture our "soul mate," everything else in life will magically fall into place. We will never doubt, never argue, never lose our initial attraction. Life will be like a storybook romance, two souls forever united in the bliss of romance.

It's a dangerous myth to buy into, and may cause more divorces than all other love myths combined. At the very least, it creates far more stress and turmoil than couples need—especially during the early years of marriage.

When Ruthie and I were dating, I had a tendency to overthink everything about our relationship. I was extremely attracted to her—both physically and spiritually—and was certain I had found my one true love. I had dated girls before, but had never been "in love," so I wanted everything to be perfect. In true Hollywood form, I began orchestrating romantic scenes and scenarios, trying to artificially create some bigger-than-life sense of connection.

Ruthie and I both loved Chinese food, so I remember buying a wok and a Chinese cookbook, then planning an elaborate dinner at my house. I bought all the ingredients we needed for fried rice and mu shu beef, then invited Ruthie over to help me cook. I imagined the two of us laughing and joking and flirting as we danced around the kitchen in "his" and "her" aprons, then afterward gazing into each other's eyes as we enjoyed a delicious dinner by candlelight. It was supposed to be the perfect romantic evening.

But it didn't turn out that way. Neither of us had ever cooked Chinese food, and the recipe book was more confusing than helpful. The fried rice turned out dry and sticky, and the mu shu beef tasted like a bowl of bad mush. We ended up throwing everything out and eating sandwiches instead. The evening was more deflating than romantic, and afterward, I remember feeling deeply disappointed. Nothing about the date turned out the way I had imagined.

Another time, I planned a romantic picnic lunch by the lake. I surprised Ruthie by picking her up on my motorcycle, my prized black and gold Kawasaki 1100. Ruthie had never ridden on a motorcycle, and I was sure she would love the thrill of gliding along the open road. I had imagined the two of us riding around the lake, taking in the fresh air and scenery, stopping along the way to play with the squirrels and snuggle against an oak tree as we enjoyed a romantic picnic dinner.

But once again, nothing went as planned. The minute Ruthie saw my motorcycle she turned white as a sheet and didn't want to get on. She was deathly afraid of motorcycles. I promised her I'd drive slowly, so she agreed to go, but she hated every minute of it. I could feel her fingers claw into my side every time I leaned into a turn. No matter how carefully I drove, she pleaded with me to go slower. We never even made it to the lake. After ten minutes of riding I turned around and took her back to her apartment.

I went home that day feeling deeply deflated and disillusioned. Nothing about the date happened as I had imagined. And I remember questioning our entire relationship. If we were truly in love, wouldn't we enjoy all the same activities? Wouldn't every moment we spent together be happy and harmonious? Wouldn't we be in perfect sync?

Because I had created so many overblown scenarios in my mind about how our relationship should look and feel, I found myself disappointed whenever reality didn't match up to my expectations. When things didn't play out in real life the way they did in my fantasies, I found myself wondering if I was with the right person. I didn't always feel in love with her, so I began to wonder if our love was real.

This habit of creating unrealistic expectations stayed with me through much of our dating relationship, and even into the first few years of our marriage. And it created a lot of undue stress and tension. I had somehow bought into the myth that love was a feeling, and when I didn't feel in love, I couldn't stop wondering what was wrong.

Thankfully, Ruthie has always been more sensible and pragmatic, especially when it came to our relationship, so she brought enough balance to the marriage to keep us from imploding. But it's a problem I still deal with today, even though I've long since learned that love is definitely not a feeling.

Myth #2: You Have a "One True Love"

Another damaging love myth perpetuated by Hollywood is the idea that somewhere in the world is our "one true love," and we will never be happy until we find them. From the earliest age girls are conditioned to seek out their prince charming, and convinced that once he comes for them, the two of them will ride away on a white horse to live happily ever after.

In the land of Disney, couples are always perfectly happy and content. There are no bills to pay, no kitchens to clean, no diapers to change, and no personality conflicts to deal with. It's all singing doves, wedding gowns and Royal Balls.

There's nothing inherently wrong with these fairy tale stories, as long as we understand that they are simply that—fairy tales. Too many young boys and girls come to subtly believe that there is a special soul mate in the world created just for them. Someone they are destined to be with. Someone designed to be their one and only true love. And believing that myth, even on a subconscious level, is a dangerous trap to fall into.

Often I (Jimmy) counsel engaged couples that have entirely romanticized views of love and marriage. During our first session together, they excitedly tell me all the things they have in common, and the many ways they are perfectly matched for each other. Usually they will hold hands and gaze into each other's eyes as they talk.

Then once they finish gushing, I begin digging deeper into their relationship, asking simple questions designed to uncover any red flags or areas of incompatibility. Often I find myself amazed at how little they really know about each other. Some of these couples have dated for months, even years, yet have never once taken the time to talk about some of the most basic issues of marriage, like where they will live, how they will pay the bills, and what dreams they have for their future.

I'm always surprised by this dynamic, but I understand the psychology behind it. On a subconscious level, couples are often afraid of bringing up issues that might strain or implode the relationship. They refrain from having conversations that they need to be having because they are afraid of where those conversations might lead. So they choose instead to focus only on the positive—on those things they have in common, and the giddy way they feel when they are together. They each want to believe that they have found their "one true love," and any idea or question that might suggest otherwise is completely rejected.

> "A RELATIONSHIP BASED ON FEELINGS IS DESTINED FOR FAILURE."

That's one of the many dangers of believing the "one true love" myth. Once you've found your soul mate, you have to hang on for dear life, because if you lose them, you may never get another chance at love.

Myth #3: Love Conquers All

One of the most surprising dynamics that I (Jimmy) have discovered in my years of pre-marital counseling is how often men and women will try to keep me from uncovering their partner's flaws and inconsistencies. Usually it's the woman who tries to hide her fiancé's faults. And when I do uncover these deeper problems or issues, they almost always come to their partner's defense and make excuses for them.

The reality is, most dating couples are well aware of each other's faults, and they've seen any potential warning signs that might have appeared. Women are especially able to recognize dangerous character flaws in the men they date. But often they choose to ignore and overlook them, even hide them from others. Instead of dealing with the problem, they tell themselves that if they can just hang on to the relationship, these issues will somehow work themselves out. That if they can just show enough love and compassion to their partner, everything will be fine.

In the world of fairy tales, love conquers all. So why shouldn't it work that way in real life?

This is a dangerous and co-dependent trap for couples to fall into. But it's far more common than you might expect.

Myth #4: Love Will Keep Us Together

At the heart of every failed marriage is the belief that two people who once loved each other are now no longer in love. If you ask either partner what happened to the marriage, their answers will always betray this truth.

"We just drifted apart." "We lost any feelings we had for each other." "Somewhere along the way, we just fell out of love."

Love was the one emotion they had in common, and it was supposed to be enough to keep them together, but it didn't work. Love failed them. It wasn't strong enough to last. It wasn't powerful enough to overcome the stress of kids and bills and failed businesses. It wasn't stable enough to keep their hearts faithful and their eyes from wandering. It wasn't meaningful enough to keep the attraction alive through wrinkled skin and graying hair. It wasn't real enough to survive the years of conflict and struggle and strife.

Love was the flame that kept their passion high, but when the spark died, their marriage died with it.

Myths Are Just Myths

When we see love as a feeling, it will always fail us, because feelings are fickle. They change with the tides. They can't be trusted. Feelings are unstable and fleeting, and almost always biased. Emotions can't be trusted. At least not for the long haul.

A relationship based on feelings is destined for failure.

Most of us understand this truth, yet when it comes to dating and marriage, far too many couples still rely on feelings as the basis for their relationship. Often they are too emotionally invested in each other and the bond they share to see things clearly—even couples who are normally very stable and pragmatic. People always believe that they are able to be objective, especially when it comes to relationships, yet very few are truly capable of it.

That's why I believe so strongly in pre-marital counseling. No couple should ever enter into marriage without first spending some time talking with a trained and qualified pastor or marriage counselor. They can bring a level of perspective and communication that simply can't be gained otherwise.

A good counselor can spot areas of potential stress and conflict, and uncover any dangerous dysfunctions or character flaws. They can ask pertinent questions that you may have never considered asking. They can help you and your partner explore any deep-seated wounds or areas of pain that might lead to serious problems in the future. And they can help bring healing to those wounds before they have a chance to do serious harm to your future marriage.

If your relationship is strong and healthy, a good counselor can give you their blessing, allowing you to go into marriage with an even greater sense of peace and confidence. And if the relationship is dysfunctional, a counselor may be able to save you from years of pain and heartache.

True Love

These are but a few of the many love myths that create stress and chaos in relationships. We'll explore other damaging myths in future chapters. But just as important as knowing what love isn't, is understanding what love is.

Love is not a feeling; it's a decision. It's not something you experience; it's something you choose to do. It's not an emotion; it's an ability. It's not something that happens to you; it's something you nurture and orchestrate and develop.

"THEY WANTED TO MAKE CERTAIN THEY WERE RIGHT FOR EACH OTHER BEFORE MOVING FORWARD."

Love is a deliberate and determined act of the will. There is nothing idle or passive about it. It doesn't wane or fail when life gets tough; it only grows stronger and more resolved. It's the bond that keeps your relationship from drifting when every storm in the ocean is raging to tear you apart. It's the one thing you can depend on when all of life seems bent on getting you down.

Love—true love—the way God intended it to be defined is the most sacred and dominant force in the universe.

It is the power of love that drove Jesus to the cross, and forever sealed Satan's eternal fate. And it's love that opened the gateway to eternal life with God in heaven.

That's the kind of love that you and I are called to bring into marriage. Not a fickle and fleeting emotion, but a resolve so strong and unrelenting that it refuses to be shaken.

Don't allow your relationships to be based on myths and fairy tale romances. Let God's love—decisive and unrelenting commitment—be the defining source and characteristic of your future marriage.

CHAPTER THREE

GREAT EXPECTATIONS

As a pastor, I (Jimmy) used to perform a lot of wedding ceremonies, and I was always honored to be asked. But I had one unwavering condition. I would only marry couples that had first agreed to pre-marital counseling—preferably with me. It was a non-negotiable policy on my end, even if I had known one or both of them for many years.

Some couples were surprised by this request, and may have even been a bit offended. They'd laugh and say something like, "You don't have to worry about us. We're perfect for each other. We've never even had an argument."

I'd usually think to myself, Now I know you need counseling!

Others quickly agreed to pre-marriage counseling and couldn't wait to show me how wonderfully prepared they were for marriage. In their minds, meeting with a pastor was just one of those preliminary things they had to do in order to get to the altar. They'd already bought the ring and picked out china patterns, so nothing was going to stop the wedding, but they decided to indulge me just the same.

Still others would agree to counseling but seemed a bit apprehensive. Maybe one or both of them had already recognized a few red flags in the relationship, and they were afraid of what problems I might uncover. They had invested so much time and energy in the dating relationship that the last thing they wanted was to be talked out of it at the last minute.

The ones I most enjoyed seeing in my office were those who came to me for counseling before planning the wedding, often before they'd even gotten engaged, because they wanted to start out their relationship on the best possible foot. They cared deeply for each other, and had already determined that they'd like to get married, but they wanted to make certain they were right for each other before moving forward. These were usually the couples that were most prepared for marriage.

Regardless of their frame of mind when they got to my office, I'm not sure any of them were truly prepared for my approach. Often couples expected to spend the time discussing all the amazing ways in which they were compatible, but my goal was to uncover any areas of incompatibility. I wanted to find out what they hadn't talked about, not what they had. I wanted to discover those issues they had been avoiding or overlooking or covering up. In short, my goal was to get them to face any uncomfortable or inconvenient issues that were bound to cause problems in their marriage, so that they could deal with those struggles before they became major sources of conflict down the road.

I've always been a no-nonsense counselor, and my approach is very direct and revealing. As a result, about twenty percent of the couples I counseled before marriage decided to break up and call off the wedding. One out of every five couples I counseled discovered things about themselves, their partner, or the relationship that they considered insurmountable. So they chose to face that truth head on and go their separate ways before it was too late.

That may sound sad to some, but it's actually a very positive outcome. Couples who go into marriage unprepared and unequipped are setting themselves up for years of grief and pain, and in many cases, a bitter divorce once these divisive issues have fully run their course. I'd much rather see those young people remain single than be married to the wrong person.

The good news is, most of the couples who did go on to get married after counseling were much more prepared and capable of building a happy life together. An extremely high percentage of the couples I counseled went on to have long and successful marriages. I've never tracked the exact percentage, but I can count on one hand the number of divorces I've seen among the couples I've counseled.

Common Sense Conversations

When counseling engaged couples, I'm continually surprised at how many basic issues of marriage they have never gotten around to discussing. Not necessarily sticky issues that might lead to embarrassment or conflict, like sex or politics, but common sense topics that you would think every couple has at least talked about.

As an example, I once counseled a very pleasant young couple that seemed perfectly happy together. She attended our church, but he went to church elsewhere. During our first session I asked them, "Where do you plan to attend church when you have kids?"

> "OFTEN THEY BEGIN LEARNING THINGS ABOUT EACH OTHER THAT THEY NEVER IMAGINED TO BE TRUE."

She perked up and said, "Well, this church, of course."

He seemed stunned by her answer. "We can't go here," he said. "I'm Catholic. We're going to my family's church."

Her mouth dropped open. "But you know I'm not Catholic," she said. "I go to church here!"

Within minutes they were in a full-blown argument. I think I was more shocked than they were. They had been dating for over a year, yet they had never once discussed where they were going to attend church once they got married.

"You realize that this is not a decision you can take lightly," I told them. "Do you know how much conflict this is going to cause in your home? If you get married without working this out, neither of you will be able to celebrate your faith without the other feeling slighted. And how do you expect to explain this differing opinion to your kids?"

After discussing the issue for almost an hour, she looked at him and said, "I love you, but I'm simply not willing to raise my kids in the Catholic Church."

He said to her, "That's a problem for me, because my family has always been Catholic. I have to be able to pass that on to my children."

Right there in my office they decided to break off the engagement. I could tell how deflated they both felt, but they suddenly realized they had reached an impasse and simply had no other choice. As bad as I felt for them, I knew they were doing the right thing.

How this delightful young couple allowed themselves to come just days away from exchanging wedding vows without discussing such a basic, fundamental issue of marriage is still a profound mystery to me. But it's a dynamic I see far more often then you might imagine.

The Dynamics of Dating

So what is it about dating relationships that keeps so many couples in the dark? Believe it or not, it's the inherent dynamics of dating that is so often the culprit.

In a dating relationship, the goal is to hide your flaws, not expose them. From the very first date, people tend to be on their best behavior. Our primary intent is to impress the other person. Often our biggest fear is that we might say or do something to drive them away, so we're constantly on guard.

A young man may have pitiful table manners, terrible hygiene, and a foul mouth when he gets angry, but send him on a date with a beautiful woman and suddenly he turns into prince charming. And he can easily keep up this façade for months if he needs to. A young woman may have deep-seated emotional problems, serious control issues, maybe even a tendency to drink too much, but when trying to impress a good-looking guy, she can seem perfectly normal.

We're all capable of putting our best foot forward when the need arises, and nowhere is that need more prevalent than when looking for a life partner.

That's why so many young people find themselves in pre-marital counseling having never discussed critical issues of marriage. They've spent so much time and energy trying to impress each other and hide their flaws that they never quite get around to discussing important life issues, like kids, bills, and differing roles in the home.

Dating is supposed to be a time of getting to know each other. A time of exploring each other's life goals and purposes, of discovering each other's hopes and expectations for marriage. A time of complete openness and honesty. A time of letting our guards down, and exposing those flawed and embarrassing parts of ourselves that almost no one else gets to see.

Dating is supposed to be a time of discovery and exploration. But too often it becomes an exercise in deceit.

Differing Expectations

When couples come to me for pre-marital counseling, one of the first things I do is hand each of them a questionnaire I call the "Marriage Expectation Inventory." It is basically a series of very simple but specific questions aimed at exploring each of their expectations in marriage, like how many children they would like to have, how their children should be raised, how they think money should be spent, who should control the finances, where they want to live, how decisions should be made, how often they would like to have sex, who should initiate sex, and who will be responsible for the daily chores of running the household. The questionnaire covers a number of different topics, many of which they may have never discussed as a couple.

Their assignment is to take the questionnaires home and complete them in private, then bring them back for our second session. I encourage them not to discuss their answers until our next meeting. Then during our second session we explore their answers together.

I never cease to be amazed at how many couples are surprised by their partner's answers. Often they begin learning things about each other that they never imagined to be true. He's always assumed they'll be moving to Alaska and she's happy right where she is. She wants to be a stay-at-home mom, and he's excited about raising their kids on two incomes. He can't wait to have sex three times a week, and twice a month seems reasonable to her.

One young couple filled out the questionnaire, and while going over their answers I noticed that he wanted six children while she only wanted two. I said to him, "So, you wrote that you'd like to have six kids. Is that right?"

"Absolutely," he answered.

Then I asked the young woman, "And you only want two kids?"

"That's right," she answered.

He looked at her with surprise and said, "I thought we had talked about this! I've always wanted six children."

Her mouth dropped open. "Not by me!" she told him.

That started an argument that went on for the next half hour. And neither of them seemed willing to bend. The issue was just one of many differing expectations we uncovered during our counseling sessions. Eventually this young couple decided to break off the engagement and go their separate ways. It was a good decision. From what I saw, they were completely incompatible, and likely on their way to an unhappy marriage, and maybe even a bitter divorce.

Healthy Expectations

Conflicting expectations can be a relationship killer. They are likely at the heart of most failed marriages. Healthy marriages are built on mutual compromise and cooperation, and when couples can't come together on the most basic decisions of marriage, they are setting themselves up for a lot of pain and frustration in the future.

That doesn't mean you have to agree on everything. But there does have to be a certain level of compatibility. For marriage to work, couples need to share the same basic views and expectations, have similar value systems, and a compatible set of goals and desires for the future. There needs to be a high degree of harmony and like-mindedness between them.

The prophet Amos asks the question, "Can two walk together, unless they are agreed?" The answer is an obvious, "No." It's impossible to walk in harmony with someone unless you are both going in the same direction. Unless you have the same destination. Unless you are traveling at the same pace. You have to have a similar mindset, and be on the same page regarding your future.

If you're contemplating marriage, now is the time to make sure you and your fiancé are agreed on the direction of your future. Have you talked openly about the details of your life together? Have you discussed the basic logistics of your future, like where you want to live, how you're going to pay the bills, who is going to work, how many kids you'd like to have, where you both see yourselves five, ten, and fifty years from now?

Do you snore? And can you sleep through someone snoring?

These are the issues that cause conflict in marriage, so these are the things you need to be discussing. No matter how mundane or unimportant they may seem to you.

If you've been dating to impress instead of to explore, now is the time to let your guards down. To talk about those embarrassing or uncomfortable subjects you've been avoiding. To share those parts of your heart—and your past—that you've kept hidden. To explore your dreams and expectations for the future.

Now is also the time to get some help at your church, or from a Christian pre-marriage counselor if you haven't already done so, even if you can't imagine needing it.

Happy marriages begin with healthy and realistic expectations. And the best time to discuss those expectations is before heading to the altar. Before differing expectations and opinions have time to become full-blown marital conflicts.

CHAPTER FOUR

WHY SO MANY MARRIAGES FAIL

No one expected Rob and Kathie to divorce after twenty years of marriage. Those who knew them best always assumed they were happy and content. They had a nice house in the suburbs and four beautiful children. And they were both involved in their church fellowship. Kathie even served as head of the women's ministry. That's why all their friends were shocked when they announced they were splitting.

I (Frank) met Rob for lunch to talk about their decision, and to see if there was anything I could do to help. It was an eye-opening experience.

"I'm just sick of being married," he said. "I love my kids, but I can't stand being around Kathie. I hate everything about her. I'm just done with it all."

Though I had known Rob for many years, I felt like I was sitting across the table from a complete stranger. His words were bitter and biting, and laced with profanities. Nothing like the gentle and kind man I had always thought him to be.

"I've never loved Kathie," he continued. "I'm not even sure why we got married in the first place. We've never had anything in common. I haven't been happy in twenty years, and I'm just tired of pretending."

I was surprised by the tone of his voice, and had never known Rob to curse, so I asked him when he began using that kind of language.

"Why, does it offend you?" he asked. "I'm not a choir boy. And believe me, Kathie is no angel either."

I had met with Rob that day hoping he would consider counseling in order to save his marriage, but it was obvious that his mind had been made up. He left our meeting just as angry and obstinate as he'd arrived.

And I left feeling both deflated and confused. How can a man throw away twenty years of marriage with such a flippant attitude? And how could I have known Rob for so many years yet never seen this side of him?

It wasn't until I had the chance to talk to Kathie a few weeks later that everything started to make sense.

"Rob is not the person everyone thinks he is," Kathie told me, her eyes swollen and weary. "He never has been. I've spent most of our marriage trying to hide that from people."

We were in a crowded room, so she kept her voice to a whisper. But I could tell she needed to talk, even though the setting was awkward. So I listened intently as she continued.

"Rob wasn't a believer when we first started dating," she said. "He only went to church with me to please my parents. He knew they would never let me date someone who wasn't a Christian, so he asked my dad to baptize him. Down deep I always knew he wasn't sincere about his faith, but I wanted to believe he would change. So I kept that hidden from my parents.

"I was just nineteen at the time, and I knew I was making a big mistake. Rob had a lot of secrets, and he thought I didn't know that, but I did. He drank too much, and would sneak away to clubs on the weekends. I thought he would change once we got married, but he never did. Things only got worse. Quite honestly, I'm surprised we lasted this long. I know now that I should have never agreed to marry him."

She leaned back in her chair and gazed into the distance with faraway eyes. Then after a long and reflective pause, she shook her head in disgust. "It's been a rough twenty years. Right now I'm just ready for it to be over so the kids and I can get on with our lives."

Why Marriages Fail

Too many couples go into marriage with blinders on. Like Kathie, they see the red flags but choose to ignore them. They know in their hearts that they are making a mistake, yet they plow forward, hoping that time and patience will win the day. But they soon discover how delusional that kind of thinking can be.

Most broken marriages are headed for failure before they even begin. It's a dynamic that I (Jimmy) have seen time and again. And as a counselor, I make it my highest priority to keep couples from making what could easily prove to be the biggest mistake of their lives.

Driven By Need

People always marry to the level of their emotional health. Always. It's like a law of nature.

Emotionally unhealthy people are like heat-seeking missiles. They have a way of finding each other. We instinctively seek out people who can fill the dysfunctional voids our emotional wounds have created.

As a young man, I (Jimmy) was deeply wounded by those who had authority over me, and I coped by developing a strong and dominant personality. I had made a number of damaging inner vows, and the primary one was to never again allow myself to be controlled. It became the guiding force of my life.

Karen was also deeply wounded at a young age, but she coped by turning inward. She became extremely shy and insecure and introverted.

In order to cope emotionally, she needed to be dominated. And I needed someone to dominate. So we found each other. Ours was a textbook co-dependent relationship, and because of it, we spent the first few years of our marriage in constant conflict.

"EMOTIONALLY UNHEALTHY PEOPLE ARE LIKE HEAT-SEEKING MISSILES. THEY HAVE A WAY OF FINDING EACH OTHER."

We were miserable, yet we were both exactly where our dysfunctions needed us to be—in a miserable relationship. Co-dependence is a strange dynamic, and yet it's one of the strongest forces in the human psyche.

A controlling and chauvinistic man will seek out a woman who is beaten down and submissive, and he will soon find a woman who meets that criterion. She will marry him because she has a deep-seated need to be controlled. An abusive and dominant woman will seek out a meek and passive man, and she will soon find him. He finds himself strangely drawn to the relationship, even though he despises the way she treats him. They need each other.

They are two incomplete people, each looking for someone else to complete them. It's a formula for a long and unhealthy relationship. And any children they have will grow up in an unhealthy home, so they, too, will likely develop many of the same dysfunctions in their own future relationships.

What Draws Us Together

We are all wounded. But we are not all defined by our wounds. That's what separates emotionally healthy people from emotionally unhealthy ones.

Healthy people have learned to overcome the pain of their past and even used it to make them stronger. They are not victims of pain; they are victors over it. They are survivors. They are not strangers to the pain that we all suffer in life, but they have not allowed that pain to define who they are. Because of it, they go into adulthood with an emotionally healthy attitude and outlook.

And emotionally healthy people are also like heat seeking missiles. They seek out other healthy people. They are not searching for a mate out of dependence or neediness. They want to build a life with someone just as healthy and happy as they are. And if that's what they're looking for, they will eventually find it.

When counseling engaged couples, my first and primary objective is to discover whether the two people sitting in front of me are drawn to each other out of dysfunctional need or healthy desire. I ask myself, Are these two healthy and rational people looking to build a life together? Or are they two incomplete people looking to each other to complete them?

The questions I ask are specifically designed to draw out any areas of dysfunction or dependence. If the relationship is an unhealthy or co-dependent one, it's my job to uncover that fact, so that I can help them avoid inevitable problems in the future.

And if the relationship is healthy, built on mutual love and respect, I'm always thrilled to give them my blessing and encourage them to move forward.

There's nothing quite as exciting as seeing two happy and healthy people enter into marriage with their eyes—and hearts—wide open. In the same way, there's nothing quite as sad as seeing two wounded and dependent people trying to fill a void that neither are capable of filling.

Assessing the Basis of Your Relationship

I'm convinced that almost all failed marriages began as dysfunctional dating relationships—even those that lasted twenty or thirty years before coming to an end. Many divorces are the result of marriages that should have never happened in the first place, because neither partner was healthy enough to build a positive and productive life with another person.

If you've found yourself in a relationship that is headed toward marriage, don't take another step forward before asking yourself some critical questions. Questions like, Why am I drawn to this person? Why am I attracted to them? What is at the root of our relationship? Am I looking to them to fill an unhealthy need or void in my life? Or is our relationship built on mutual dreams, interests, and attractions? Are they emotionally healthy and happy? Am I?

Take time for some deep and honest soul searching about yourself, your partner, and the underlying basis of your relationship. Are the two of you equally yoked spiritually and emotionally? Do you share common life goals and visions? Why do you want to spend the rest of your life together?

This is also a good time to involve people you trust in the process. If you haven't searched out godly counsel and advice, why not do that now? What do your friends and family think of your relationship? Do you have your parents' blessing and approval? If not, why not? Do they have a reason to be leery of your relationship?

And have you sought spiritual guidance and direction? Is God at the center of your relationship?

If you haven't made a regular habit of praying with and for your partner, now is the time to start. Ask God to reveal any hidden flaws and dysfunctions in both you and your partner's character. Ask him to guide you as you seek his will for your future. Pray that he will open your eyes to any relational red flags or areas of incompatibility. Pray for his will to be done, then commit to listening and heeding the Spirit's voice when he speaks.

God has a wonderful plan for your life, and that plan most likely includes a long, happy, and fulfilling marriage. So trust him with your future, follow wherever he leads, and I promise you will never be disappointed.

CHAPTER FIVE

THE RIGHT (AND WRONG) WAY TO DATE

Someone recently asked kids between the age of five and ten a series of questions about love and marriage. Some of the answers they gave were as funny as they were enlightening.

Glenn, who was seven, had a pragmatic approach to love. "If falling in love is anything like learning how to spell, I don't want to do it. It takes too long."

John, age nine, had a similar reaction. "Love is like an avalanche where you have to run for your life!"

Mae, also age nine, had a more romantic outlook. "No one is sure why it happens, but I heard it has something to do with how you smell. That's why perfume and deodorant are so popular."

Mike, age ten, wasn't so idealistic. "On the first date, they just tell each other lies, and that usually gets them interested enough to go for a second date."

Mike may understand the problem better than most.

Andrew, age six, had a pretty good understanding of what brings couples together. "One of the people has freckles, and so he finds somebody else who has freckles too!" Sounds reasonable to me.

But when it comes to marriage and commitment, no one nailed it quite like Marlon, age ten. "A man and woman promise to go through sickness and illness and diseases together."

If that isn't true love, I don't know what is.

When asked about the rules of dating, Jim, age ten, came right to the point. "You should never kiss a girl unless you have enough bucks to buy her a big ring and her own VCR, 'cause she'll want to have videos of the wedding."

And Tammy, age ten, seemed to agree with him. "It's never okay to kiss a boy. They always slobber all over you. That's why I stopped doing it!"

I'm glad she stopped.

The most practical, no-nonsense answer, however, came from Howard, age eight. "The rules go like this: if you kiss someone, then you should marry her and have kids with her. It's the right thing to do."

Howard just might grow up to be the next pastor of your church. And trust me, you could do worse!

The Rules of Dating

When it comes to dating and marriage, there seem to be as many ideas on the subject as there are people on the planet. We all have our own thoughts about what is and isn't proper etiquette when guys and girls start to pair off. Even in Christian circles there is a lot of room for disagreement and debate. And it's not hard to see why.

Try searching the words "dating" or "courtship" in your online Bible and you'll come up empty-handed. In fact, scripture doesn't appear to address the topic at all—at least not directly. That's because the concept of dating didn't exist in biblical times, and still doesn't exist in many Middle Eastern cultures. When the Bible was written, marriage had little to do with compatibility or personality traits. Unions were arranged based on family lineage, religious background, and economic status—more about creative bartering than falling in love. As a result, the Bible seems to be relatively silent when it comes to choosing a marriage partner.

That doesn't mean that we can't look to Scripture for solid advice on the subject. The Bible speaks volumes about relationships and godly interactions between men and women, and those principles can clearly be applied to dating and courtship.

I've been speaking and teaching on marriage for much of my adult life, and the principles I teach come directly from the pages of Scripture. The Bible gives clear direction and guidance on building a strong and healthy marriage. When marriages fail or suffer, it is almost always because couples have ignored these biblical principles and instead defaulted to self-centeredness and insensitivity. When we ignore God's warnings, our lives suffer.

"WHEN IT COMES TO DATING AND MARRIAGE, THERE SEEM TO BE AS MANY IDEAS ON THE SUBJECT AS THERE ARE PEOPLE ON THE PLANET."

That same dynamic holds true when it comes to dating relationships. The Bible gives a wealth of instruction and advice on what healthy relationships look like, and the importance of sexual and moral purity. And couples who ignore these warnings in their dating relationships are bound to suffer.

There is a godly way to date, and that is what you want your relationship to look like if you are seeking God's guidance and direction. God speaks when we are obedient. That's true in every area of the Christian life, and especially true when it comes to seeking his will for our future.

Let's take some time to look at what a healthy and honorable dating relationship looks like.

Built on Honor and Respect

I (Frank) have no regrets about marrying Ruthie, but I have a number of regrets about the way I courted her. If I could go back and do it again, there are a lot of things I would do differently.

First, I would have shown her father more respect by including him in the process. Ruthie and I were both in our mid-twenties when we met, so I never saw the need to ask her father's permission to date her, or even to marry her. In my eyes, Ruthie and I were both adults, old enough to make those decisions on our own. I realize now that it was wrong of me to assume that.

The Bible tells us, "Honor your father and mother… that it may go well with you and that you may live long in the land."

God commands us to treat our elders with respect and honor in all things, and it was wrong of me to court Ruthie without first seeking her father's blessing and approval. Regardless of her age at the time, he was her protector, both physically and spiritually. He was more than her biological father; he was her spiritual covering, and he deserved the honor of being consulted in every area of our relationship. I didn't do that, but I wish now that I had.

I also should have been more respectful to Ruthie. As a suitor, it was my job to court her properly and guard her heart, instead of playing with her emotions.

Paul commanded Timothy to treat "younger women as sisters."

In many ways, my dating habits were selfish and inconsiderate. Though I knew what a prize Ruthie was, I was too insecure to show my hand and let her know that. Dating felt more like a game to me, so I was never honest about how I felt about her. I was afraid to commit to the relationship, and had a habit of dating other girls at the same time I was seeing her—like a newly-licensed driver shopping around for the best deal on a new car.

We were both committed to virginity, and we remained true to that commitment. But there were other boundaries I should have set in place as well. By the time we got married, we were emotionally wrung out—especially Ruthie. I'm not sure why I was so childish and immature, or why Ruthie stayed with me, but my lack of respect for her feelings nearly imploded our relationship before it had a chance to begin.

Too many young people see dating as a recreational sport. This is especially true with teenagers, who are too young to commit to a serious relationship. To a hormone-driven sixteen-year-old boy, a "sport" is all dating can really be (which is one reason I highly discourage teenagers from dating).

But when young people become more established, and reach the age where they are seeking a marriage partner, dating should take on a level of intentionality. The purpose of dating is to find a life partner, someone who shares our interests and values, someone who possesses the kind of spiritual and moral character that we desire in a future spouse. Someone that we enjoy being with, and who enjoys being with us.

Dating is a process of discovery and openness. And the people we date deserve to be treated with dignity and respect. The relationship should be one of mutual honor and honesty and commitment.

Equally Yoked

It's always a curious thing to me when Christian singles agree to date non-believers. Why would anyone who is a follower of Jesus believe that they could build a happy and healthy relationship with someone who doesn't share their views and values on the most important life decision they have ever made? It is a monumental mystery to me, yet I see it all too often.

Paul warned the believers at Corinth, "Do not be yoked together with unbelievers. For what do righteousness and wickedness have in common? Or what fellowship can light have with darkness? What harmony is there between Christ and Belial? Or what does a believer have in common with an unbeliever?"

I'm not sure God could speak any clearer on the issue. When it comes to marriage, it's nothing short of insane to think we could somehow build a life with someone who doesn't share our spiritual beliefs and practices.

"Missionary-dating" may sound like a noble endeavor, but it is in direct opposition to Scripture, and can never be justified. It is always a bad idea.

If you've found yourself dating a non-believer, you are in direct disobedience to God's will. There is no way to sugarcoat the issue. And that is a dangerous place to be.

> "IF YOU'VE FOUND YOURSELF DATING A NON-BELIEVER, YOU ARE IN DIRECT DISOBEDIENCE TO GOD'S WILL."

Physically and Mentally Pure

Not so long ago, most people understood that sex before marriage was a bad idea. Even those who didn't profess to be Christians knew that premarital sex was immoral. People still did it, but they usually kept it hidden. Today that isn't the case. Over the past few decades, we've seen a concerted effort to redefine the moral code of our culture, blurring the lines between right and wrong. Today, sexual promiscuity is not only accepted; it is expected. And those who hold traditional and moral values are shunned and ridiculed for being "old fashioned."

As a result, even Christians seem to have become confused on the issue. In a recent survey conducted by ChristianMingle.com, Christian singles between the ages of 18 to 59 were asked, "Would you have sex before marriage?" The results were both sad and sobering. Sixty-three percent of respondents answered "yes."

Oddly enough, in the same survey, Christian singles were asked how important "praying and going to church" was when looking for a future spouse and the vast majority answered "highly desirable."

In far too many circles, Christian singles have somehow compartmentalized their faith from their sexual purity. I'm not sure when this fog of confusion settled onto the Christian dating scene, but it is a dangerous trend. And it's in direct opposition to God's Word.

Time and again scripture warns against sexual immorality, including pre-marital sex.

> "It is God's will that you should be sanctified: that you should avoid sexual immorality; that each of you should learn to control your own body in a way that is holy and honorable, not in passionate lust like the pagans, who do not know God; and that in this matter no one should wrong or take advantage of a brother or sister. The Lord will punish all those who commit such sins, as we told you and warned you before. For God did not call us to be impure, but to live a holy life."

> "Flee from sexual immorality. All other sins a person commits are outside the body, but whoever sins sexually, sins against their own body. Do you not know that your bodies are temples of the Holy Spirit, who is in you, whom you have received from God? You are not your own; you were bought at a price. Therefore honor God with your bodies."

> "Let marriage be held in honor among all, and let the marriage bed be undefiled, for God will judge the sexually immoral and adulterous."

There is no ambiguity in scripture when it comes to the dangers of sexual immorality. If God had outlined some hard and fast rules for dating, I'm certain that sexual purity would be at the top of the list. Healthy dating relationships, above all else, should be defined by clear sexual and emotional boundaries.

Within the context of marriage, sex is a beautiful and sacred thing. It is perhaps the most spiritually and emotionally bonding activity a couple can engage in. Sex holds marriages together. It creates a oneness of heart, mind and body. And it's a wonderful thing for single people to anticipate.

But sex outside of marriage is not only sinful; it is ugly, detached and disruptive. It is disrespectful, both to God and to each other. And it can do more damage to your future relationship than we truly comprehend. Once you allow yourself to compromise sexually in a dating relationship, you've opened yourself up to a host of other compromises.

Author Shaunti Feldhahn has done extensive research on the topic of sex and dating, and she found that couples who engage in sex before marriage are far less happy and content than those who wait. Nearly seventy percent of men who cross that line say they no longer feel they can trust their partner. And eighty-two percent of women become deeply insecure in the relationship, saying it causes them to become clingy and emotionally needy.

God's laws are not randomly derived. There is a reason he calls us to sexual purity. And even if we don't understand the reason, as followers of Christ, we should be willing to obey.

How Healthy is Your Relationship?

There is a right and wrong way to date. And if you've found yourself dating the wrong way, I encourage you to put the brakes on and put in place some clear new boundaries and habits.

If you sense an air of disrespect and dishonesty in your relationship, if you haven't fully committed to honoring your partner and his or her family, if you've found yourself playing emotional games, or your partner seems to treat dating as a recreational sport, then you have the power to put an abrupt end to it. Have enough self-respect to say, "This is not the relationship that I signed on for. This is not what God wants for me! This is not the kind of marriage that I plan to have!"

If you've found yourself dating an unbeliever, someone who doesn't share your spiritual values and beliefs, I strongly encourage you to put your relationship on hold until that changes. And if it doesn't change, save yourself years of grief and heartache by ending the relationship altogether.

If you've allowed yourself to cross lines of sexual and emotional boundaries that you know God expects you to maintain, then decide today to change your course. Explain to your partner that you will no longer engage in sexually impure activity, and make sure they know you mean it. If they agree with you, then put in place some clear physical restrictions in order to keep your relationship pure. If they respect you and share your values, they will welcome the new boundaries. If it causes them to leave, then trust me, you are far better off without them.

If you and your partner are headed toward marriage, now is the time to set the tone for your future together. Because the tone you set will have a marked impact on your relationship for many years to come.

Strong marriages begin as healthy dating relationships. And the healthier you date, the greater chance you have for a long and happy marriage.

CHAPTER SIX

INTENTIONAL DATING

I (Jimmy) have a friend who designs jewelry for the rich and famous. He told me once that in one day he saw three different clients who each planned to spend over a million dollars on their weddings. All three of them forked out a small fortune for their rings, and appeared to be putting more effort into picking the jewelry than focusing on the strength of their upcoming marriage. He told me he didn't expect any of those marriages to last more than a few months.

A professional photographer who does work for us at MarriageToday told me recently that he increasingly finds himself delivering wedding photos to couples who are already divorced. That's why he's learned to get full payment up front.

There's a disturbing trend in our culture today that I've noticed for some time. People are putting an inordinate amount of time, money, and effort into planning their wedding ceremony, and very little into the health of their courting relationship. I think I know where this trend originated, though it's just a theory. Like many damaging trends in our culture, I believe this one originated in

Hollywood.

Many decades ago, the trend in Hollywood among the rich and famous was to simply "shack up" with each other. Television and movie stars had a dim view of marriage, so they simply began living together in revolving door relationships. That trend funneled down to society during the 70s, 80s, and 90s, and that's why cohabitating has become such a common practice. The "movers and shakers" of society made it seem acceptable, and the masses naturally followed suit.

Then a few years ago, Hollywood stars decided that marriage had come back in style. I remember reading an article about the resurgence of marriage among the Hollywood elite, and we've seen that play out in real life. Today it's impossible to turn on the news without hearing of another "A List" celebrity couple planning to get hitched. Famous couples are getting married in record numbers, and then competing to see who can put on the most elaborate and expensive wedding. To help offset the cost, they hire private photographers and sell the photos to any tabloid willing to fork out the most cash.

Of course, most of these marriages last about as long as a Tootsie Roll, but that doesn't stop them from trying.

Once again, this new trend has funneled down to the rest of our culture. We've seen a resurgence in the number of couples getting married the last few years, and many of these couples are trying to emulate the rich and famous by throwing the biggest and best weddings they can afford. Many of them can't afford it, but they go into debt in order to make it happen.

And just like their counterparts in Hollywood, a growing number of these marriages are ending in divorce, simply because they've been so focused on planning an impressive ceremony, that they never took time to build a strong foundation for the marriage.

Again, that's just my theory. But I think it holds water pretty well.

The problem is, elaborate ceremonies don't make for happy marriages. It is the quality of the courtship that determines the strength of the relationship, not the extravagance of the wedding ceremony.

The Right Way to Date

If there is a trend that needs to take hold in society, it is a trend toward healthy and intentional dating relationships. Because once the ceremony is over, you still have to build a life together. You're just as married, whether you spend five hundred dollars or five million dollars on the wedding. Planning a ceremony is the easy part. It's navigating life together that can bring grown men to tears.

My (Frank's) daughter Kandilyn just got engaged to a wonderful young man named Bryson. They'll be getting married before the end of this year, and I couldn't be more excited for them. Their courting relationship may be as healthy and purposeful as any I've ever witnessed.

The two met in a small group Bible study about a year ago. Bryson says he was immediately smitten with Kandilyn, and he let her know that within a few weeks of meeting her. Kandilyn was attracted to him, but she wasn't ready for a dating relationship, so he had to settle for being relegated to the "friend zone." They ran in a lot of the same circles, and were both involved in several campus ministries, so they spent a lot of time together, but only as good friends. They soon became close friends. Bryson knew what a prize Kandilyn was, so his interest in her never waned.

"IF THERE IS A TREND THAT NEEDS TO TAKE HOLD IN SOCIETY, IT IS A TREND TOWARD HEALTHY AND INTENTIONAL DATING RELATIONSHIPS."

Because the two of them were spending so much time together without the pressure or pretense of dating, Kandilyn was able to see Bryson's true character and personality. It wasn't long before she realized what an awesome and godly young man he was. He eventually won her heart, so she agreed to date him. That's when Bryson asked to meet me for coffee in order to ask permission to date my daughter.

"I don't believe in casual dating," he told me. "I don't think it's right to play with a girl's heart that way. But I've gotten to know Kandilyn really well over the months, and I'm interested in pursuing a relationship with her. She's the type of girl that I hope to marry some day, so I'd like your permission to court her, so we can get to know each other better."

He went on to explain what their dating relationship would look like, including the physical and emotional boundaries he would be setting in place. He was intent on keeping their relationship pure and wholesome, without even the appearance of impropriety. In fact, they had already discussed the matter, and both were committed to reserving their first kiss for the wedding. The more he talked, the better I felt about him.

I gave them my blessing, and then kept a close watch over the coming months to see how they navigated their courting relationship. I couldn't have been more impressed. Instead of going out to movies every night, they spent much of their time sitting in our quiet living room, talking, asking each other questions about their dreams for the future, their likes and dislikes, their expectations in the way of family and career and spiritual development. They spent time memorizing chapters of the Bible together, and praying for wisdom and guidance.

Almost every night we could hear them talking and laughing from the other room as they whiled away the hours getting to know each other on an intimate, heart-to-heart level.

They also spent a lot of time volunteering for evangelistic events and projects, so they were able to see how well they got along during times of busyness and stress. They went on grueling winter hikes with their friends, allowing them to interact during times of pressure and fatigue and physical exhaustion. They spent time with both his family and ours in order to see how well they each interacted with the other's parents and siblings. They constantly looked for new ways to interact in different settings in order to get to know each other better.

After months of intentional dating, Bryson met with me again to ask my blessing as he prepared to propose to Kandilyn. Then just last weekend, he planned an elaborate picnic in a nearby park at sunset, where he dropped to one knee and asked for her hand in marriage.

It rained cats and dogs that night, but I'm not sure either of them even noticed.

Why Intentional Dating is Important

Kandilyn and Bryson are well prepared for marriage. Though they are bound to face areas of conflict and struggle, as all couples do, I'm confident they'll be able to navigate those problems more easily than many couples, simply because they have spent so much time building a solid foundation for the future.

Their relationship is based on a shared faith, goals, and values. They are not star-crossed lovers, driven to marriage by overactive hormones. They are two best friends deciding to build on that friendship and create an intentional and covenantal future together.

If more couples took this type of intentional approach to dating, there would be far more healthy and happy marriages. And rates of divorce would likely drop to the single digits.

So what does it take to build a truly healthy and intentional dating relationship? Though there are many important dynamics at work, there are a few key principles that need to be set in place in order for your dating relationship to be successful. These principles are more than good ideas; they are critical to growing a truly Christ-centered, God-honoring, purposefully pure relationship with your potential mate.

Commit to Honoring God

There is a marked difference between a Christian dating relationship and a secular one, and that difference should be easily apparent to others. When Christians date, everything they say and do as a couple should be honoring to God, first and foremost. Before they even take steps to establish a relationship, they should spend time in prayer, asking God for confirmation and blessing as they set out to get to know each other better.

Bryson and Kandilyn were both raised in strong Christian homes, and they instinctively understood this principle. At the very beginning of their dating relationship, they committed to honoring God in every decision. And as their relationship developed, they continued to seek God for wisdom and guidance as they navigated their courtship together. Even now as they set out to plan the wedding ceremony, they lift up every decision in prayer before moving forward.

"THERE IS A MARKED DIFFERENCE BETWEEN A CHRISTIAN DATING RELATIONSHIP AND A SECULAR ONE."

When couples set out to honor God first with their relationship, it creates an entirely new dynamic between them. God not only guides their courtship, but he helps them navigate areas of struggle and temptation. He honors their faithfulness by playing an intimate role in their daily interaction.

Set Clear and Healthy Boundaries

Physical and mental purity is essential to a healthy dating relationship, and the way you maintain purity is through clear and defined boundaries. And there's more to a pure relationship than simply not having sex. A truly pure courting relationship means maintaining purity of heart, mind, and body.

There is no shame in having healthy sexual desires. The shame comes when you allow yourself to act on those desires and engage in impure thoughts and activities. Many Christian couples date with the best of intentions, but they soon fall to temptation because they haven't put into place some clearly defined boundaries.

Bryson and Kandilyn committed early in their relationship to some very stringent boundaries in their courtship. They decided to not allow themselves to be alone in any type of private or intimate setting. They have never once been alone in either of their bedrooms, and never hang out in each other's homes unless others are there with them. They do this to not only alleviate unwanted temptation, but to ward off even the appearance of impropriety.

They decided to go one step further and refrain from kissing until their wedding. And any type of physical petting or caressing is strictly off limits. They didn't set these boundaries because they thought kissing or physical affection before marriage was somehow wrong or sinful. They simply understood how easy it is for godly, well-intentioned young people to give in to temptation, and they were committed to entering marriage with no regrets or emotional baggage.

The boundaries that Bryson and Kandilyn set in place are based on their own personal convictions, and may be different than the boundaries you choose to set. But the intended outcome should be the same. Your goal should be to do whatever it takes to keep your relationship sexually and mentally pure, and only you know what boundaries need to be implemented in order to make that happen.

Keep Yourself Accountable

Bryson lives in a house with four other Christian guys, and their primary role as roommates has been to hold each other accountable. They made this clear when they moved in together, and they have stayed true to that commitment. They are a great community of friends, and I'm proud of their commitment to God and each other as they keep each other spiritually and physically pure—not just in their dating relationships, but in every area of life.

One of the best ways to keep your relationship healthy and pure is to surround yourself with people who are willing to hold you accountable. And then give them permission to ask you any question that they feel needs to be asked. Share with them the boundaries that you have set in place, and then ask them to confront you any time they see you pushing the limits of those boundaries.

Good accountability partners can do more than keep you from falling to temptation. They can help you go into marriage with a pure conscience and an unblemished reputation.

Have Intentional Conversations

Instead of spending all of your time talking about the latest movies or where you hope to go on your honeymoon, use the time you spend together to discuss issues that define your core values. Talk about your relationship with God, and what He has done to shape and mold your spiritual character. Pray together for guidance and wisdom as you navigate your courtship. Keep a journal of your prayers so that you can look back and see how God has answered those prayers. Discuss your hopes and dreams for your future family.

The things you discuss while dating will have a marked impact on your future. And these conversations need to be deliberate and intentional. Dating should be fun, but it should also be seen as a means to an end. Your goal is to learn all you can about each other's true inner thoughts and character. To discover if you are equally yoked, and compatible. To see if you share the same spiritual values and beliefs. To determine if this is the person you are willing to commit to for the rest of your life.

It takes intentional conversations to build a healthy and intentional relationship.

Seek Godly Guidance and Counsel

The difference between wise people and foolish people is that wise people listen to good advice when they get it. And they're willing to heed that advice, even when it seems counter-intuitive.

In many dating relationships, couples tend to isolate themselves from others and spend all of their time alone—often gazing longingly into each other's eyes. But healthy couples seek out other healthy couples to mentor them along and guide them in their relationship. They understand the importance of mentoring and being mentored, in every area of life.

One of the wisest things you can do during a dating relationship is to allow others to speak into your life. Spend time with your parents, or any married friends who have shown to have a strong marriage. Look to them to help you work through any areas of conflict or concern. Talk to your pastors or elders about any struggles you may be having. Seek advice from those you trust to give you godly counsel, and allow them the freedom to confront you if they have any concerns about your relationship.

Too often, the only advice dating couples get comes from their other single friends. And that's just the blind leading the blind. When you need good advice on building a strong relationship, you're far more likely to find it with people who have already navigated the waters you're trying to sail.

Continue to Evaluate the Relationship

Perhaps the most admirable thing I've seen Bryson and Kandilyn do over the course of their courtship is to regularly re-evaluate their relationship. Several times during their courtship they made a conscious decision to sit down and talk about how things were progressing. They made a pact early on to be brutally honest with each other during these discussions, and to share any concerns or misgivings they may be feeling. And they decided that if either of them felt that the relationship wasn't working for them, the other would honor those feelings, and the two would part friends.

Obviously, that never happened, but the fact that they were willing to have these purposeful discussions showed a great deal of wisdom and maturity on their part. And it did a lot to strengthen the bond they were building, and bring even greater security to the relationship.

If the purpose of dating is to evaluate whether you want to spend the rest of your life together as a couple, then some serious discussions regarding your future need to take place. And those discussions need to feel safe and honest and purposeful. There is no shame in deciding to end a relationship if it isn't working. The shame would be to never have those kinds of candid discussions, and to feel pushed into a marriage that you aren't quite sure you want.

Healthy Skills for the Future

Many of the same principles for building a happy marriage apply when setting out to build a healthy dating relationship.

It takes two people willing to be honest with each other, and committed to honoring God with their relationship. It takes healthy boundaries, and a covenantal commitment to doing whatever it takes to keep your relationship pure and undefiled. It takes a willingness to hold yourself accountable—not just to each other, but to those you trust to keep you pure. It takes a high level of communication with deliberate conversations in order to work through areas of conflict or disagreement. And all of that works best when you surround yourself with godly friends and mentors who can give you solid counsel and advice.

Learning to date with intention and purpose is a good idea, because those principles will also help you build a strong and healthy marriage. They are good habits to learn now, and will build skills that will prove invaluable in your future marriage.

CHAPTER SEVEN

THE TEN COMMANDMENTS OF ONLINE DATING

According to an October 2013 report by Pew Research, 11% of American adults and 38% of those who are single have tried online dating, or an online dating mobile app. This same report showed that 66% of online daters have gone on a date with someone they met through a dating site or a mobile app. And 23% of them say they have met a spouse or long-term partner through these sites.

Online dating continues to grow in popularity and many people have had positive experiences with it. I tend to be neutral on the subject. It is a great tool for those who want to meet someone, as long as they do so in a wise manner.

I (Jimmy) know of many couples that met online and have very happy marriages. I also know of single people who have had very bad experiences with online dating.

One such person is a woman we'll call Sandra. She was in her forties and had been previously divorced. She had gone for several years without dating until a friend finally convinced her to try online dating. After a few days of looking at profiles and communicating with men online, Sandra set up a date with a man who matched her desires and seemed like someone she'd like to get to know better. We'll call him Dan.

When Dan asked for Sandra's address, she was hesitant, but decided to give it to him since his profile described him as a devout Christian. He had described himself as being active in his local church and having a strong Christian faith, so she reluctantly gave him her address and anxiously waited for their first date the next weekend.

Dan showed up Friday night at 7:30 p.m., just as they had arranged. Sandra peeked out her bedroom window as he walked to her door, impressed by how handsome and clean cut he was. He looked exactly like his profile picture, which was a big relief.

She greeted him at the door and invited him in. Sandra was nervous because she hadn't dated in such a long time, but she worked to keep her composure. Dan stepped into the door and Sandra turned to grab her purse, then as she turned back around Dan surprised her by leaning in to kiss her on the cheek. He put his hand on her shoulder and she could feel his fingers brush against the top part of her chest.

It was an awkward moment, and Sandra took a step backward.

"Wow, I didn't expect that!" she said. She nervously reached for the front door, wanting to leave as quickly as possible. Dan followed her out the door, but with a slight hesitation, as if he wasn't quite ready to leave. Sandra, however, couldn't get to the car fast enough. She wasn't offended by Dan's kiss; she just wasn't sure how to process what had just happened.

The conversation in the car on the way to the restaurant was polite and positive, and Dan seemed interesting and funny. But he continued touching her on the hand and arm, which made her a bit uncomfortable. It seemed a little odd to her, and a bit too familiar. Then just before pulling up to the valet parking, he patted her on her upper thigh as he assured her that this was the best restaurant in town.

Sandra tried to hide her frustration as they walked into the restaurant, but Dan's behavior was starting to wear on her nerves. And he didn't seem to catch on to her non-verbal signals. Even as the hostess greeted them, he had his left hand on her lower back with a couple of fingers brushing the top of her buttocks.

The hostess seated them at their table and Sandra quickly excused herself, making her way to the restroom, just to get away for a minute and think about what she should do. She didn't want to ruin her date, but she also wasn't sure how to respond to Dan's forwardness. Am I being a prude? She thought. Maybe this is how everyone dates and I've just been out of the scene too long. Regardless of how she tried to justify Dan's behavior, something inside of her felt violated, and she didn't feel comfortable being touched so inappropriately.

After gathering herself in the restroom she returned to their table.

"Is everything okay?" Dan asked.

She assured him she was fine, and they continued making small talk. But Dan continued touching her hand from across the table. Halfway through dinner he moved his chair so that the two were seated side-by-side, and as he did, he once again placed his hand on her upper thigh. She quickly scooted her chair away from him, so he drew back his hand and moved away.

As they talked over the next hour or so, Sandra began to feel more comfortable. Dan became less forward, and the conversation turned light and familiar. They talked about the Lord, about Dan's job, her job, their families and a myriad of other subjects. The more they talked, the more at ease Sandra began to feel.

After dinner, the band began playing and couples started making their way to the dance floor, so Dan asked Sandra if she would like to dance. The music was from the 40's and 50's, and seemed slow and romantic, so Sandra agreed.

The two began dancing, and within a few minutes Dan had pulled Sandra tightly against himself with his right hand. Sandra was once again on high alert as Dan slowly slid his hand down toward her buttocks. She grabbed his arm and moved it away, but he was un-phased. Rather than getting the message, he moved his hand higher and began to massage her upper back.

Just before the song ended, he once again moved his hand back down toward her upper buttocks. But this time, he pulled her toward him and began dancing in a very sexual manner. There were so many people on the small dance floor that no one noticed, but Sandra was mortified.

When the song ended she told Dan she was ready to go home. He begged her to stay but she refused, so they drove silently back to her house. Dan stopped at a park about a block from Sandra's house and told her he just wanted to talk. Then without notice, he began forcing himself on her. He repeatedly groped and grabbed her, thrusting his body on top of her. Sandra instinctively knew that she was about to be raped.

She was somehow able to fight Dan off and get out of the car, then ran as fast as her legs would carry her. Afraid that Dan might be chasing her, she began looking for houses with lights on, or people who might be able to help, but the streets were empty. Finally she made it to her front door and looked back just in time to see Dan driving away.

Sandra sobbed uncontrollably that night, and called her best friend Linda to see what she should do. She decided not to call the police unless Dan contacted her again. Thankfully, he never did. But she did report his behavior to the dating website and they cancelled his membership. The episode terrified Sandra so much that she didn't date again for several years.

Sandra's story may not be typical, but it's worth telling, because there are very real dangers to online dating. I should stress again that many people have had positive online dating experiences, so I don't mean to paint it with a negative brush. But there is an inherently dangerous dynamic to online dating that should be taken into consideration.

In most dating relationships, couples generally know each other better before the first date. Often they know each other from work or school, and probably have a lot of the same friends. They may be from the same community, and know each other's general reputations in the community. They may even know each other's parents and siblings, and have a good idea of their family dynamics.

But that is seldom the case with online dating. When you meet someone online, all you know about them is what they choose to share in their dating profile. You don't know their friends, their family, their reputation, or anything else about them. You also don't know how they treat their parents, or how sincere they are about their faith in Christ.

That doesn't mean that you can't get to know those things, only that you have to be careful and use a great deal of caution and wisdom. Otherwise, like Sandra, you could find yourself on a very awkward date with the last person you'd ever want to meet in a dark alley.

Not All Experiences are Bad

Not all online dating experiences are negative. I (Frank) know a young girl who met an incredible young man on a Christian dating site. She was already out of school and simply wasn't in a position to meet many good Christian men her age. She attended a small church, and wasn't interested in any of the guys she had grown up with. She was a beautiful young girl who worked at a coffee shop, so guys were constantly hitting on her, but they all seemed to be the wrong kinds of guys.

At the prompting of a friend, she hesitantly signed up for an online dating site, and within a few months had met a great Christian man from a small town in Texas. She lived in Colorado, so they had to navigate a long distance relationship, but they made it work, and were able to spend a lot of time together as they got to know each other better. Today they are happily married, and recently had their first child.

> "ONLINE DATING CONTINUES TO GROW IN POPULARITY AND MANY PEOPLE HAVE HAD POSITIVE EXPERIENCES WITH IT."

For people who don't have a lot of opportunity to meet others, online dating can be a great option—as long as you understand the dangers and pitfalls, and approach it wisely. To help you do that, we've put together our Ten Commandments of online dating to help keep you out of trouble. These are ten critical things to remember if you choose to give online dating a try.

The Ten Commandments of Online Dating

One: Be careful

Don't believe everything people write on their online profiles. It's easy to fudge the truth and make yourself look better than you are when trying to get the attention of others. Some people who date online are desperate. Others may be predators. Not the majority, of course, but enough to give you reason to be suspicious. So be careful, and don't believe everything you read.

Two: Be realistic

No matter how compatible with someone you appear to be on paper, there are inevitable problems and issues you will have to work through. Your perfect soul mate won't be perfect. You will have different needs, different perspectives and may still have to work through baggage from the past. Don't be deceived into believing that matching profiles will automatically lead you to a "happily ever after" ending. Compatibility is not based on similarity or sameness. It is something you build through shared values, character, faith and culture.

Three: Be honest

When communicating online, be honest about yourself. If you try to be deceptive, you'll eventually be found out. And any online matches you appear to have won't be true matches. Online dating won't work if you aren't truthful. This includes using honest, un-photoshopped pictures of yourself, and truthful answers to every question they ask.

Four: Take it slowly

The very nature of online dating demands that you take things slowly and cautiously. Unfortunately, many people who date online do the exact opposite. They convince themselves that matching profiles is a guarantee for success, so they tend to move forward much too quickly. Once they meet someone and find the initial date positive, they're ready for marriage. But the primary purpose of dating is to see your potential mate's character over a long period, and under a lot of different circumstances.

Are they moral or immoral? Are they kind or abusive? Do they honor their parents? Are they going to love me for a lifetime or start taking me for granted? Am I going to stay first in their lives, or are they going to put their friends or work before me? Are they sincere about their faith in Christ? Are they faithful in attending church? Are they good with money?

These are the questions you need to be asking regardless of how you meet someone, and it takes time to know these things for certain. Maybe not years, but a minimum of several months. It's true that no two couples are the same, but every couple needs adequate time to truly get to know each other's true inner character before signing on for a lifelong relationship.

Five: Meet in public the first few times

Don't make the same mistake that Sandra made and give your address to a complete stranger. What Sandra should have done was agree to meet Dan at a restaurant for their first date. She would have had her own car, and he would never have learned her address. She would have likely known halfway through dinner that Dan wasn't the guy she thought he was, and the episode in his car never would have happened.

The best approach is to always meet someone in a neutral, public setting for the first few dates. At least until you know them well enough to trust yourself alone with them.

Six: Meet the first time in an unromantic setting

No matter how well you think you know someone from your online chats, it's a mistake to meet in a romantic setting before getting to know their true character. Your first meeting should never allow the chance for physical contact or romance. That might sound prudish, but it is good advice. The best place for a first meeting would be a busy coffee shop or a casual diner—a place where you can sit and visit with little opportunity for romance or unwarranted intimacy. This gives you the opportunity to size them up and get to know them before things get more familiar. You will have no regrets if you take things slowly and methodically.

> "YOU WILL HAVE NO REGRETS IF YOU TAKE THINGS SLOWLY AND METHODICALLY."

Seven: Don't be sexual

One of the biggest red flags to watch for when dating online is over-sexualized language and photos on personal profiles. These are intended to attract attention, but don't allow yourself to be drawn in by them. Men are especially vulnerable to contacting women based on seductive profile pictures, but it's a huge mistake. Sensual photos may work in advertising, but in an online profile it's an almost certain sign of low self-esteem and poor character.

The purpose of dating is to find someone with strong convictions and a healthy inner character. You also want someone who shares your Christian faith and values. People who use sex and seductiveness to attract others are not the kind of people you want to date. Any relationship they build will be as shallow as they are.

Eight: Never date unbelievers

When believers date unbelievers for the purpose of evangelizing them into the kingdom, it's called "Missionary dating." It is never a good idea, it rarely works out, and it is unbiblical.

I (Jimmy) have counseled dozens of heartbroken husbands and wives in unequally yoked marriages, and they deeply regret not placing a higher value on their faith. You shouldn't even consider dating a non-believer—or even a marginal believer. Make sure that anyone you agree to go out with is a committed believer with an active and genuine faith. It's also important that they share your spiritual beliefs and theological convictions. You're not just dating; you're looking for a future spouse, and you need to be able to agree on what type of church you will attend when raising kids together.

This commandment is not a suggestion. It is critical to your spiritual future and your ongoing relationship with God.

Nine: Date one person at a time

People who date online often date more than one person at a time, but that's not a healthy approach. It is fine to look at a number of profiles and to chat with as many people as you desire, but once you decide to start going out, only date one person. If there are others you have an interest in dating, you should be honest about that. It may be exciting and flattering to have multiple relationships going on at the same time, but it seldom ends well. Focus on one serious relationship at a time, and don't date again until the present relationship has ended.

Ten: Verify important information

I know a woman who completely deceived her fiancée about her true character. Soon after the wedding, he discovered that she was a complete fraud, and that nothing she said about herself was true. It was his own fault for being too naïve and trusting. When someone makes claims online, it's important to verify those claims before agreeing to date them.

Verifying facts is not that hard these days, so take time to do it. Do they actually work where they claim to work? Do they have any children they haven't told you about? Are they making child support payments they "forgot" to mention? Are they financially secure, or deep in debt? Are they truly single? Are they secretly living with someone?

These are all serious things you need to know about someone, because they will have a marked impact on your future, should you decide to move forward with the relationship. If their bio checks out, you can put your mind at ease. If it doesn't, you know they can't be trusted.

Keeping Things In Perspective

The most important thing to remember when attempting to meet someone online, is that all the same rules apply, regardless of how you choose to date. Whether you meet someone at church, at work, at school, or an online dating site, you still have take a measured approach and get to know all you can about them before deciding to move forward.

You need to get to know their parents and friends, and see how they interact in different social settings. Are they respectful to their parents? Do they get along with their siblings? Are they from a healthy family? Are they loyal to their friends? And do those friends hold them in high regard?

Most importantly, do they have a strong faith in God, and a lifestyle of honesty and integrity? And, do they have the character and personality traits that you're looking for in a future spouse?

Treat online dating the same as you would any other type of dating relationship, heed these Ten Commandments of Online Dating, and hopefully your experience will be positive and rewarding.

CHAPTER EIGHT

RECOGNIZING RED FLAGS

I (Jimmy) once counseled an engaged couple and during the first meeting noticed an interesting dynamic. Every time I asked the young woman a question, her fiancé would answer for her. This went on for the entire hour.

I asked her how many bridesmaids she was planning to have at her wedding. Before she had time to answer, he said, "She's going to have six." She seemed surprised to learn that.

Over and over this happened. No matter what question I asked, he would answer for her. I was starting to get irritated, so I looked him squarely in the eye and said, "Excuse me, but I'm talking to her."

He folded his arms across his chest and let her answer the next question, but after that he was right back at it.

It only took a few sessions for me to realize what a bully he was, and I warned them that he was dominating the relationship. Several weeks into counseling I encouraged her to break off the engagement, or at least put it on hold until he could get some counseling to work through his need to control, but she didn't listen. They went forward with their plans to marry. I haven't seen them in awhile, but I guarantee she's miserable, and likely afraid of her husband.

Their relationship was one of the most co-dependent ones I'd ever seen, and I wish I could have convinced them to wait.

So many couples go into marriage with huge red flags hanging over their heads. And the longer they date, the larger these red flags grow. Often these couples seem completely oblivious to the danger signs that everyone else seems to be able to see. They either choose to look the other way, or are far too invested in the relationship to care.

But these red flags are signs of almost certain disaster and pain once the marriage vows have been spoken. They all but guarantee years of struggle and conflict and dysfunction. The time to heed these warnings is before the wedding, while there is still time to head off trouble.

> "MARRIAGE ONLY WORKS WHEN BOTH PARTNERS WORK AS A TEAM."

These relational red flags take on many different shapes and flavors, and it would be impossible to cover every warning sign a couple should look for when evaluating their relationship. But let's take time to discuss some of the more prevalent and dangerous ones I've witnessed through the years.

Control Issues

Issues of control and domination may be the most common problem I see during premarital counseling. It was the primary issue that Karen and I faced during the early years of our relationship, and it very nearly destroyed our marriage. It would have if God hadn't stepped in and changed my heart and actions.

Control issues can vary in degree, from simply wanting to be in charge of the relationship, to a need to control every aspect of a partner's life, like what they wear, what they say, who they talk to, where they go, and what they are doing every minute of the day. These severe issues of dominance are easy to spot, and extremely dangerous situations for the weaker partner. In these cases, I encourage couples to break off the relationship and each get serious counseling on their own.

But more common are those subtle issues of control that aren't that easy to expose. One partner is strong-willed while the other is somewhat passive, and the relationship is one-sided. This often works during the dating phase because the passive partner simply allows the other to make most of the decisions. But once they get married, this quickly becomes an area of tremendous tension and conflict.

And control issues go both ways. While most of the time it is men who are the dominant partners, I've seen a lot of relationships where the woman is the controlling force.

Marriage only works when both partners work as a team. When one is making all the decisions, the other quickly begins to feel slighted and disrespected. So they begin rising up and trying to regain some say in the relationship. Simple decisions regarding money or meals or children suddenly turn into a battle of wills. The stronger partner doesn't like feeling challenged, so they become even more controlling and dominant. It's a fast track to an early divorce, unless they get professional help.

Physical or Verbal Abuse

Not all controlling relationships become abusive, but when they do, it quickly turns into a dangerous and volatile situation. Abuse, in any form, can never be overlooked or taken lightly, and it always gets worse.

The most common form of abuse in dating relationships is verbal. And it tends to begin rather subtly. One partner begins joking about the other, or putting them down, and these verbal attacks slowly escalate. It's almost as if they are gauging how much verbal abuse the other is willing to take without leaving. Little by little, their attacks get more personal and vicious. Soon they find themselves in a full-blown verbally abusive relationship.

Bullies have a way of finding victims. And their bullying tactics tend to get worse as time goes by. Verbal abuse is often a precursor to physical abuse.

If you've found yourself in a verbally abusive dating relationship, my advice is to put the brakes on now, before it is too late. Don't delude yourself into thinking it will get better once you are married, or that you are somehow the one at fault.

This is one red flag warning you can't afford to ignore.

Anger Issues

Often, when counseling engaged couples, our conversations will be going rather smoothly, then suddenly I'll ask a question that seems to strike a nerve. Both will grow suspiciously quiet. So I'll ask a follow-up question on the same topic. Again they grow quiet. One will laugh and try to change the subject, but I don't let them. I realize that I've touched on a delicate issue, and the way they react often speaks volumes about any problem areas they might be hiding.

It's during these awkward moments that anger issues tend to rise to the surface. I sense that I've come across a topic that one—or both—of them is afraid to bring up, and there's usually a reason for that. Often it's because one is afraid of how the other will react. All I have to do is watch their body language and I know immediately which partner is the one struggling with anger.

The biggest problem with anger issues is that they are easy to hide from friends and family, and both partners have a tendency to keep it hidden from others. It's an embarrassing issue to deal with, both for the victim and the offender. And since we all get angry from time to time, saying someone has a "problem" with anger is a subjective judgment. And no one wants to be judgmental.

But anger issues are a big deal in the context of marriage, and they need to be identified and dealt with before standing at the altar. Otherwise, you could be setting yourself up for a lot of pain and conflict.

Dishonesty

I (Frank) once knew a young man who was engaged to a beautiful girl, and they seemed like the perfect couple. But there was always an air of distrust between them. She often accused him of flirting with other girls, and he found himself keeping close tabs on her. This lack of trust soon became the defining characteristic of their relationship.

One day I confronted the young man about it and learned that he had caught her seeing other men several times while they were dating. Though she apologized for her behavior, he never felt that he could trust her again. And because of her breach of trust, he found himself secretly monitoring her emails and text messages, and this caused her to lose faith in him. She didn't think he could be trusted, either.

They eventually broke off their engagement and went their separate ways. And that was a good decision, because trust is a precious resource, and you can't build a healthy marriage without it.

When couples catch each other lying, or harboring secrets, it puts an enormous strain on the relationship. Trust is an imperative ingredient to marriage. It is the foundation of safety and security that you have to have in order for the marriage to stand. Without it, you have almost no hope of building a strong and healthy marriage.

If you can't trust your partner to be honest with you while dating, don't kid yourself into thinking that it will somehow change after you're married. It will only get worse.

A Pattern of Conflict

It's always a curious thing when couples who can't seem to get along decide that they want to get married. As if they are somehow eager to take their fighting to the next level. But I see it all the time. And too often, they don't seem to be able to recognize this as a problem.

When couples have a pattern of conflict, it's usually a sign that they are incompatible. They are better off splitting and finding a more harmonious partnership. These couples are seldom happy when I (Jimmy) bring this up during counseling, but it's my job to make happy marriages, not more friends. Most couples that are in constant conflict simply shouldn't get married, even though they don't want to admit it. Often they've invested so much time and energy in the relationship that they can't imagine starting over.

In these situations, I tell couples, "You have two options. Either you can get married and plan on spending a lot of time in counseling, learning how to get along and resolve your arguments, or you can break up now and part as friends. Then you're both free to find partners that better fit your temperament and personality." It's harsh, but it's the truth.

That isn't always the case, though. Sometimes I run across couples who seem to be compatible in almost every way, and they truly care about each other, but just can't seem to resolve conflicts when they arise. Often this is because they simply haven't learned how to have a fair fight. There is a right and wrong way to resolve conflict, and it's something any couple can learn. In these cases, I spend time teaching them the basic skills and techniques of conflict resolution, and it almost always revolutionizes their relationship. Often these couples go on to have the strongest and most vibrant marriages.

> "WE'RE ALL SOMEWHAT IMMATURE BEFORE MARRIAGE, AND YOUNG PEOPLE NEED TIME TO DEVELOP THEIR SKILLS AND CAREERS, SO YOU CAN'T EXPECT YOUR POTENTIAL MATE TO BE FULLY ESTABLISHED."

If you've found yourself in a pattern of conflict with your potential mate, only you can decide whether it is a basic sign of incompatibility, or a simple inability to resolve conflict. But don't kid yourself into thinking it is normal. Constant bickering is not a typical part of dating. It's a sign that something between you is not working. And the time to resolve that problem is before the wedding, not after.

Overdependence on Parents

More than ever before, I've begun to see a very real "failure to launch" dynamic among today's young people. And there are many reasons behind it.

When the economy is stagnant, as it has been for many years, young people give up looking for work and instead find it easier to live in their parents' basement. Children also tend to stay in college longer, and some use education as an excuse to postpone the responsibilities of careers and families and bills. Some young people are simply lazy and indifferent, and accustomed to being taken care of by their parents.

Whatever the cause, the trend is very real. And I see the effects often during premarital counseling. A growing number of young people today tend to be more immature and dependent on their parents, but that doesn't keep them from wanting to get married. It does, however, create a host of different problems when they do.

Overdependence on parents, or a lack of independence, is a huge red flag issue to watch for, especially in young men in their early to late twenties. If your fiancé is still living at home, still being supported by his parents, maybe in a state of arrested adolescence, it's a bad idea to assume that he will suddenly grow up once you get married. If you're a young woman who dreams of being a stay-at-home mom, make sure you're marrying a man who can help you fulfill that dream.

And it goes both ways. If you're a young man dating a girl who is still dependent on her parents, who isn't expected to cook or clean or do the laundry, who couldn't survive without her parents' help, you may be in for a surprise.

We're all somewhat immature before marriage, and young people need time to develop their skills and careers, so you can't expect your potential mate to be fully established.

In many ways, marriage turns boys into men, and it turns girls into women, so anytime there's a wedding, there's a lot of maturing that still has to happen. But there should be a certain level of independence established once children reach college age and beyond. If you're concerned that you may end up living with your fiancé's parents, it may be time to step back and reevaluate.

Mood Swings

If your potential mate finds it difficult to express emotions, or is prone to extreme mood swings, it would be a good idea to assess the cause. Maybe they are happy one minute, laughing and joking, and then suddenly turn sad and sullen the next. Or maybe they are given to unexpected bouts of fear, insecurity, sickness, or paranoia.

Unstable emotions can be annoying during the dating phase, but in marriage, they can be devastating to a relationship. Learning to be newlyweds is emotionally challenging in any scenario, but trying to navigate your new life with an emotionally unstable partner can be nothing short of maddening.

Some people may struggle with a manic depressive personality. If so, they need to be diagnosed and treated. Others may simply have grown up in an angry and dysfunctional home, and that's the only model they know. They've become addicted to chaos. Still others are simply wired to be emotional, and struggle to keep their mood swings in check.

Whatever the cause, if you worry that this might be a problem, deal with it now, while there's still a level of rational thinking.

An Air of Disrespect

If you sense that your partner is treating you with disrespect, that's not a feeling you should ignore. Maybe they make little jokes at your expense, or tend to tease you with sarcasm. Perhaps they criticize you in front of friends, or use belittling language when they're angry. Or maybe they just blatantly talk disrespectfully to you.

This is not something you can overlook. Sarcasm is not funny; it is textbook passive-aggressive behavior. Below the surface there is always a level of contempt and condescension. Joking and belittling language is far from harmless. It is blatant bullying, and always grows worse with time.

A rude and disrespectful fiancé is going to turn into an angry and contentious spouse. Don't allow yourself to put up with it.

Dysfunctional Family

All families deal with a certain level of dysfunction. We are imperfect people, saved by grace, and expected to extend grace to those around us. If you run across a seemingly perfect family, run as fast as you can, because they're likely hiding bones in the basement.

You can't expect your fiancé's family to be perfect, but you can hope for a certain level of normalcy and function. Highly dysfunctional families have a way of breeding dysfunctional children. It's impossible to get through childhood without being affected by the way your parents act and react.

I know a young woman who grew up in an extremely angry and volatile home. Her father was a certified rageaholic, who would terrorize his family at the slightest infraction. This young girl was deeply wounded by her father, and swore she would never treat her children that way. She got engaged to a young man in her twenties, and married shortly afterward. During their courtship she seemed perfectly normal, and never once lost her temper. She was insecure and emotional, but never showed signs of rage. Until after the wedding. Just a few months into the marriage, she became a physical and emotional bully, blowing up at the slightest argument. She acted exactly as she had seen her father act.

Because of her dysfunctional upbringing, she became a ticking time bomb, just waiting for the right time to explode.

You can't assume that your fiancé will become just like his or her parents, because we all have our own personalities. But don't discount the power of a dysfunctional childhood. To some degree, we are all a product of our past, and some of us are more affected by our past than others. So be wise, and make sure you're going into marriage with your eyes wide open. A dysfunctional family isn't a reason to break off an engagement, but it's certainly a red flag you need to be aware of.

Trust Your Intuition

Obviously, this is not intended as a comprehensive list of red flags to watch for, but it's a good place to start.

Ultimately, when it comes to recognizing relational red flags, you have to trust your instincts. If you have a general uneasy feeling about your partner or your relationship, that's a feeling you shouldn't ignore, even if you can't quite put your finger on the problem. Intuition is a compass that guides you, and keeps you out of trouble when things aren't quite what they seem.

Sometimes there is an indefinable uneasiness that settles into our spirits, and we can't get past it. That happens in business, in ministry, in financial decisions, when buying a new car, in almost every area of life. And it happens in relationships as well. Often that uneasy feeling is God trying to get our attention.

If everything about your relationship looks good on paper but still leaves you feeling anxious and concerned, it might be the still small voice of the Holy Spirit speaking to your heart.

Then again, it might be cold feet or a bad slice of pizza, but you won't know for sure unless you take time to seek God's guidance and do some reevaluation.

Listen to your instincts when you sense something is wrong. Whether that means getting counseling, putting your relationship on hold, or ending it altogether.

Marriage is one decision in life that God expects you to get right the first time. So don't allow yourself to be rushed. And don't make a mistake you'll regret for the rest of your life.

SECTION TWO

Preparing to Build a
Happy Marriage

CHAPTER
NINE
HEALTHY COMMUNICATION

A young dating couple named Josh and Sarah are on their way to dinner one evening, enjoying their favorite song on the radio, when suddenly Sarah perks up and says, "Josh, do you know what today is?"

"No, I don't," he answers.

"It's August 1st," she says excitedly. "That means it's our six month anniversary! Our first date was on February 1st. I remember because it was the day before Groundhog Day."

Josh nods and smiles, then reaches over to change channels on the radio. He silently keeps driving.

Sarah notices that he didn't respond, so she thinks to herself, Maybe I shouldn't have brought that up. Maybe he thinks I'm being pushy. He didn't remember, so maybe it's not that important to him. Maybe I'm not that important to him? Maybe he's starting to doubt our relationship? Am I being too clingy? Am I turning him off? Am I getting too serious about our relationship?

And Josh is thinking, August 1st. That means hunting season is just a few weeks away! I wonder if I need to stock up on ammo?

And Sarah is thinking, Why did I do that? I'm always moving too fast and pushing guys away. But it's not like I asked him to marry me! I'm just excited about our anniversary. You'd think he would be excited too. If he really liked me, he would have been the one to remember! Six months is a long time to be dating! Doesn't he see that?

And Josh is thinking, I think I have some .243 ammo left over from last year. It's probably in the back of the gun cabinet.

And Sarah is thinking, You know, he's not so much of a prize either! Maybe I'm the one who should be questioning our relationship? Maybe I'm the one who needs to find someone else?

And Josh is thinking, I should call Fred in the morning to see if he still has that deer blind set up.

And Sarah is thinking, Why do I always waste time on men who won't commit to a serious relationship? I don't deserve to be treated this way! If he doesn't want to be with me, then maybe it's time to move on and find someone who does! I'm so done with men who refuse to grow up!

So Sarah says, "I don't feel like going to dinner tonight, and apparently you don't either! Why don't you just take me home?"

And Josh says, "Are you sure? What's wrong?"

And Sarah says, "What's wrong? You have to ask me that? Don't act like you don't know! Just take me home this minute!"

So Josh takes Sarah home, completely baffled and confused. All the while thinking, What in the world just happened?

Mars, Meet Venus

Sound familiar? I'm certain it does, because we've all experienced the differences between men and women when it comes to communication.

Years ago someone wrote a book titled, Men are From Mars, Women are From Venus, and it became an instant best-seller, because everyone could instinctively relate to the title. We've all had gender-mixed conversations that felt like we were trying to communicate with someone from another planet.

In spite of what the feminist movement has tried to convince us, men and women are very, very different. And we are different in almost every area of life—how we think, how we feel, how we react, how we connect, how we process information, how we grieve, how we compete, how we solve problems, how we see the world around us. We look different. We act different. We are different.

And nowhere are we more different than in the way we communicate.

Men tend to communicate in order to relay information. We generally talk more about topics than feelings and emotions. Men are wired to be highly competitive, and tend to focus more on solving problems than discussing them.

Women, on the other hand, communicate in order to connect. They would rather discuss their feelings than things or topics. They are more relational and intuitive, and their speech reflects this truth. Women tend to be more concerned with nurturing people through a crisis than finding a way to solve it.

If you were to walk into a crowded room and announce, "There's a fire on the third floor of this building," the majority of men and women in the room would have very different reactions.

Most of the men would immediately think, Where is a fire extinguisher? Which way to the nearest stairwell? What is the quickest way to get people off that floor? Their first instinct would be to solve the problem.

But in that same moment, most women would instinctively think, Where are my children? How did this happen? I wonder if I know anyone on the third floor? We have to pray that no one gets hurt! Their initial reaction is rooted in empathy and concern.

"WE ARE DIFFERENT BECAUSE GOD WIRED US THAT WAY. WE ARE CREATED TO COMPLEMENT EACH OTHER, TO WORK AS A TEAM, TO BRING BALANCE INTO RELATIONSHIPS, TO COMPLETE EACH OTHER."

We are different because God wired us that way. We are created to complement each other, to work as a team, to bring balance into relationships, to complete each other. In the context of marriage, our differing temperaments and personalities bring steadiness and stability to the family.

In marriage, men and women become one in heart, but we are still very different in substance. Like two sides of the same coin—each uniquely fashioned, but equal in weight and significance.

And that's reason for celebration, because it can bring a lot of fun and excitement to the relationship. But it can also bring cause for fear and trepidation—especially for couples about to navigate the inevitable storms of marriage.

Ingredients For Healthy Communication

Successful marriages are not the result of two people who happen to be just like each other. They are the result of two very different individuals who understand their differing views and personalities, and have learned to communicate well enough to work through their differences.

Most people might believe that being "soul mates" is the key to building a happy marriage, but the fact is, good communication is what makes the difference. It is through healthy and effective communication that couples learn how to become soul mates.

When counseling engaged couples, I (Jimmy) can usually tell within the first thirty minutes of the first session how successful they are likely to be at growing a strong marriage. And it isn't because they happen to have similar personalities, or because they enjoy the same views and interests, or even because they appear to have some special connection with each other. What I look for is good communication skills. How they speak to each other, how they listen when the other speaks, how well they've learned to talk through issues and conflicts. I watch how they communicate their needs and feelings, how they relay their wants and desires, how effective they are at expressing their point of view and understanding their partner's viewpoint.

Couples who understand the power of words and the dynamics of healthy communication are the ones I know are equipped to build a long and successful marriage relationship.

And couples who don't are likely in for a huge surprise once the wedding bells have faded and the reality of sharing life with another person has settled into full swing.

Communication is the bridge that gaps the inherent differences that men and women bring into marriage. And for communication to be healthy and effective, it must include four key ingredients. These are the elements of communication that every marriage needs in order to survive and thrive. They can help build a good marriage, and they can repair a severely damaged marriage. And they are what separate happy relationships from dysfunctional ones.

These four critical ingredients to healthy communication are: Caring, Praise, Truth, and Faith.

Communication Ingredient #1: Caring

Caring is the first key to effective communication, and likely the most important. It's impossible to communicate with someone who doesn't care what you need or desire, and ultimately doesn't really care what you have to say.

"COMMUNICATION IS THE BRIDGE THAT GAPS THE INHERENT DIFFERENCES THAT MEN AND WOMEN BRING INTO MARRIAGE."

An atmosphere of caring is what usually brings dating couples together. It's the magnet that first draws us, and the glue that keeps us engaged in the relationship.

When Karen and I (Jimmy) first stated dating, I listened to everything she had to say, because I wanted her to like me. I set out to learn all I could about her: what she liked, what she didn't like, what made her happy, what made her sad, what she liked to eat, what kind of movies she liked, where she wanted to go on dates. I listened because I cared about her, and everything I did and said reflected that truth. I was young and infatuated, so I set my sights on wooing her into a relationship.

But after a few years of marriage, when we were struggling to get along, that was the primary thing that changed. I stopped showing her how much I cared. Instead of listening intently when she talked, I would tune her out, or roll my eyes, and basically disengage. I stopped caring, and it very nearly destroyed our marriage.

When God stepped in to save our marriage, the first thing he expected me to change was the way I acted toward her. He convicted me to start caring again. To listen when she talked. To care about what she had to say. To truly care about her needs and desires and opinions. To begin treating her the way I did when we were dating.

Relationships die in an atmosphere of apathy and self-centeredness. And they blossom in an atmosphere of caring and concern.

Caring is the bellwether trait of a strong and vibrant marriage. And it takes more than words to communicate that you care. Caring is communicated through actions, through body language, through a caring tone, through eye contact, through intentional times of conversation and dialogue, through truly listening to what the other is saying, and then changing what needs to change in order to meet your partner's needs. Caring is putting another's needs above your own. And it is the first critical ingredient to healthy communication.

Communication Ingredient #2: Praise

Negativity is the devil's language, and it will destroy your life if you let it. It will destroy your health, your career, your friendships, your dreams, your hopes for the future, and every relationship you have. It will also devastate your marriage. Nothing good and healthy can exist in an atmosphere of pessimism and discouragement.

But praise is a wellspring of hope and happiness and optimism. It is a gateway to intimacy. An atmosphere of praise causes people to open up their hearts and spirits, while an atmosphere of criticism causes them to shut down emotionally.

Imagine going on a date with someone who constantly criticized you. They criticized your hair, your clothes, your weight, even the way you held your fork. They belittled you for slouching at the table, or slurping your soup, or talking too loud. Everything they said was couched in negativity.

Would you ever go on a second date with them? Not if you had an ounce of self esteem, because no one likes to be criticized.

Now imagine yourself married to such a person. Would you be happy and content? Of course not.

Strong relationships are built through the language of praise and affirmation, and that's how good marriages grow even stronger. The defining quality of every great marriage is a positive tone and attitude. It is the central characteristic of every successful and fruitful relationship.

Communication Ingredient #3: Truth

The apostle Paul tells us to "speak the truth in love." And that is another key ingredient to effective communication. There's nothing loving or compassionate about speech that isn't couched in truth.

Too often couples traffic in deceit in order to keep the peace. When something is bothering them, or they have an unmet need or desire, they choose to keep it to themselves instead of risking conflict. They would rather seethe in secret than confront the issue head on. But that's not only unhealthy; it's dangerous. Unmet needs breed contempt and resentment. And unhealed wounds only grow and fester.

You can hide a skunk in the basement, hoping no one will notice, but eventually it's going to stink up the entire house. The same is true with untended wounds and offenses. When we bottle up our pain and bitterness, it will eventually rise to the surface, and usually manifest itself in the form of passive-aggressive behavior.

In marriage, learning to speak the truth in love is a critical step to keeping resentment at bay. If there is something you need, something your partner has done to offend you, or something about your relationship that isn't working for you, it's important to communicate that truth to your spouse.

Honesty strengthens a marriage, while deceit only strains it.

Communication Ingredient #4: Faith

It is possible for a couple to have a good marriage without a foundational faith in God, but I don't believe such couples can ever have a great marriage. Faith brings a level of purpose and meaning to marriage that simply can't be found through any other means.

When a relationship is built on Jesus and centered on Christian values and beliefs, it takes on a higher level of significance and value. It becomes a union of hope, commitment, and substance. It becomes more than an earthly journey; it's an eternal one.

God becomes the center of the relationship, and everything revolves around honoring God's will and desire for the marriage.

Faith also becomes the focal point of our communication. Couples are not communicating to simply relay information or to work out problems, but to keep the marriage on track spiritually. Couples communicate with each other, and then come together to communicate with God. Every decision becomes a three-way conversation, and ultimately, every decision rests with God.

When couples surrender everything they say and do and think to God, it transforms everything about their relationship. It changes the way they speak to each other, the way they look at each other, the way they interact as a couple, the things they do for each other, and the way they honor and cherish each other.

Communication that is faith-based and God-centered is the greatest form of communication a marriage can have. And it's what I see at the heart and soul of every really successful marriage relationship.

Communication is a Skill

Communication problems are like ticking time bombs. You never know when they're going to go off and wreak havoc. Couples who don't learn to communicate effectively are destined for years of heartache and strife, and in many cases, a long and bitter divorce.

But couples who do learn to communicate well, and develop the skills they need to truly connect with each other, almost always have the happiest, most fulfilling marriages. They quickly discover the joy and purpose that God designed marriage to bring.

The good news is, healthy communication is a skill that anyone can learn. It's not a natural thing for many of us, but a critical set of skills if you ever hope to have a great marriage. And the time to develop those skills is before you get married, not during the heat of your first major conflict—and trust me, if you plan to get married, you can expect some serious conflict in your near future.

The primary purpose of healthy communication is to help you resolve conflicts when they arise, before they have time to do irreparable harm to your marriage. And that takes a level of skill and patience and understanding that few of us are born with.

That's a topic we'll tackle in the next chapter.

CHAPTER TEN

EFFECTIVE CONFLICT RESOLUTION

I (Jimmy) once counseled a young couple that wanted me to marry them. We'll call them Paul and Rita.

Rita told me that they almost never argued, but she was worried about Paul, because whenever conflict would arise he would get very quiet and go off by himself for a few hours. When he came back he seemed fine.

I gave them both a Taylor Johnson Temperament Analysis, which is a test I use to gauge personality traits and compatibility. When I got the tests back, I was stunned to see that Paul had scored 100% in the "anger" category. I had seen high scores before, but nothing quite like that.

I said to him, "Are you aware that you scored 100% in the anger category?"

He seemed surprised by the result. "No, I didn't know that," he said.

So I asked him, "Who are you angry at, Paul?"

"I'm not angry at anyone!" He answered.

Rita smiled and chuckled. "Yes, you are. You beat yourself with wrenches when you get mad."

"I don't do it all the time," Paul said.

"You do it a lot," she responded. "He also puts people in the hospital when he plays football!"

"You put people in the hospital?" I asked him.

"Well, not on purpose," he said, leaning back in his chair. "I'm a linebacker, so it's my job to hit hard, and sometimes I get a little aggressive, but I'm not trying to hurt anyone."

I paused for a few seconds, then asked him again, "Paul, who are you mad at?"

"I'm not mad at anyone," he said again.

So I decided to get more specific. "Are you mad at your coach?"

"No."

"Are you mad at Rita?"

"No."

"Arc you mad at people of other races?"

"No."

"Are you mad at your school?"

"No."

"Are you mad at the government?"

"No."

I went down the list of everything I could imagine that might be causing Paul's anger. Until I got to his family.

"Are you mad at your mother?" I asked.

"No, I love my mother."

"Are you mad at your father?"

Suddenly his demeanor changed drastically. "I'll kill that man if I ever see him again!"

I was pretty sure I had stumbled upon the problem.

"So tell me about your father," I said.

"He left my mother when I was young, and I swore I would never let him in the house again. I'll kill that man if he ever hurts her again."

Paul spent the next ten minutes talking about all the ways his father had hurt him and his family, and the struggles they went through after his father left. I could sense the anger welling up in his spirit.

"Paul, you have to find a way to forgive your father," I told him. "Otherwise, your anger is going to eat you alive."

He locked eyes with me and clinched his jaw. "There's no way I'll ever forgive that man. Not after what he did to us."

I gave him a few minutes to calm his spirit, then said to him, "Whether you know it or not, this anger in your spirit is destroying any hope you have of being happy, or building a healthy marriage. Your anger is holding you hostage, and because of it, you will always be miserable. Every time you hit someone on the football field, it's your father you're trying to hurt. Every time you hit yourself with a wrench, the blows are intended for your father. Your need for revenge is tearing you apart, and I guarantee it will destroy your marriage if you don't deal with it now."

Paul became very quiet and lowered his head. Then without warning he started to cry. His tears were slow at first, but soon became uncontrollable. He couldn't stop. And it seemed to go on forever. Rita embraced him, doing all she could to comfort him, but the tears kept flowing.

Paul cried like a baby for a solid sixty minutes. Then suddenly he lifted his head, wiped his eyes one last time and said, "Okay, I know I have to forgive him, so I'm ready."

I asked Paul to bow with me as I led him in a prayer of forgiveness, asking God to take away the anger and give him the strength to forgive his father. Paul repeated each word as we prayed together.

The next week Paul and Rita came back for a second counseling session and the minute they sat down, Rita said with a smile, "Paul is a completely different person. We can't make him mad. I've tried all week, but it won't work. We used to have to walk on eggshells around him, but now we don't have to. I've never seen him this happy and calm."

Over the coming weeks I was continually amazed at how different Paul had become. He was completely healed of his anger. Once he finally surrendered his anger and forgave his father, God was able to heal him from the inside out. Paul and Rita went on to get married, and as far as I know are still doing well today.

A Powerful Lesson

Not everyone who prays for healing is delivered from their pain the way Paul experienced, but I've seen such miracles before. God did that same miracle in my heart many years ago, and it saved our marriage. It's always an amazing thing to witness.

But the primary reason I wanted to share Paul and Rita's story is to relay a powerful truth that any person contemplating marriage needs to remember. It's actually one of the most powerful words of counsel I could possible give—and may be the most important truth you take away from this book.

And that truth is this: when you marry someone, you are not just marrying the person you've fallen in love with. You are marrying their pain. You are marrying every wound they've ever suffered at the hands of another person. You are marrying their abusive and neglectful father, their overbearing mother, their angry and alcoholic uncle, their hurtful and offensive grandfather. You're marrying the boss that overlooked them for a promotion, the business partners who cheated them, the third grade teacher who embarrassed them in front of the entire class.

> "WHEN YOU MARRY SOMEONE, YOU ARE NOT JUST MARRYING THE PERSON YOU'VE FALLEN IN LOVE WITH. YOU ARE MARRYING THEIR PAIN. YOU ARE MARRYING EVERY WOUND THEY'VE EVER SUFFERED AT THE HANDS OF ANOTHER PERSON."

No matter who you marry, or how well adjusted they have become, you are no doubt marrying a host of hidden and unhealed wounds from their past. And those wounds are bound to show up at one time or another.

Obviously, some of us bring less emotional baggage into marriage than others. Not all of us are products of abuse or neglect or an unbearably painful upbringing. But we are all products of our past, no matter how healthy or unaffected we appear to be. We all carry a certain level of dysfunction into marriage. And nowhere will our dysfunctions be more apparent than in the ways we deal with conflict.

Healthy Conflict

Conflict in marriage is not necessarily a bad thing. In fact, healthy conflict is actually a sign of a strong and vibrant relationship. The couples I worry most about are those who say they never argue, because they are likely avoiding conflict. Maybe they're afraid of making waves, so they keep their unmet needs and feelings to themselves. But we all know that it's impossible to navigate life with another person without some level of struggle and friction, so pretending it doesn't exist is not a solution. It's actually an indicator of a much bigger problem.

Healthy relationships are not those that avoid conflict, but those that learn to effectively and lovingly resolve conflict when it arises.

Dr. John Gottman is a clinical psychologist who has done extensive research on the dynamics of marriage. His studies on the causes and preventions of divorce have proven to have a ninety- four percent accuracy rate when predicting which couples will divorce within three years of their initial interview.

After more than twenty years of research on the subject of marriage and divorce, Dr. Gottman concluded that the key to a strong marriage is not the absence of strife and struggle, but a healthy approach to resolving problems when they arise.

He writes:

> *"If there is one lesson I have learned from my years of research it is that a lasting marriage results from a couple's ability to resolve the conflicts that are inevitable in any relationship. Many couples tend to equate a low level of conflict with happiness and believe the claim 'we never fight' is a sign of marital health. But I believe we grow in our relationships by reconciling our differences. That's how we become more loving people and truly experience the fruits of marriage."*

If a couple isn't arguing, they aren't working through their differences. And that only leads to bottled-up anger and resentment. In the worst cases, it leads to apathy and indifference, which is the sign of a seriously distressed marriage.

Healthy conflict is the result of two people fully invested in growing a strong and vibrant relationship. You both want the marriage to work, so you're willing to do whatever it takes to resolve any hint of discord.

Intimacy is borne of struggle. It is a law of the universe. There can be no fire without friction, no growth without growing pains, no forward progress without movement. It is through struggle that we learn how to be fully engaged in the relationship.

Steps to Conflict Resolution

So what does healthy conflict resolution look like? What does it mean to have a fair fight in marriage?

There are many dynamics to effectively resolving conflicts, and it would take an entire book to fully explore the topic. But let's take a Reader's Digest look at the subject. I (Jimmy) have spent the last thirty plus years helping couples resolve their differences, and in my experience, couples who are the most successful at overcoming conflict are those who practice these basic principles of conflict resolution.

Whether you're still dating or have been married for fifty years, these simple principles are critical to developing a strong and vibrant relationship.

Principle #1:

Overcome your fear of confrontation. No one enjoys confrontation. When left with a choice, almost all of us would prefer to avoid conflict instead of meeting it head-on. But in marriage, that's an unhealthy approach.

For marriage to work, there has to be a high degree of communication. And nowhere is communication more important than when we encounter a problem or an offense. When Satan wants to destroy a marriage, he begins by cutting off the lines of communication. Satan doesn't want couples to talk; he would rather them seethe in anger. Because when we aren't talking about our problems, we're allowing them to grow and build.

When you feel slighted by your partner, or you have a need that is going unmet, or you sense you've offended them in any way, the most loving thing you can do is go to them and say, "We need to talk."

Principle #2:

Give each other the right to complain. In order for you and your spouse to feel safe and comfortable talking about problems, you both need to have permission to complain. Karen knows that if I've ever done anything to offend her, or if there is anything I'm doing—or not doing—that hurts her feelings, she can tell me about it with absolutely no fear of retribution. She knows that I will listen, and that I won't hold it against her. She can tell me anything, because I have given her that right. And she has done the same for me.

It wasn't always that way between us. There was a time when she would never have come to me with an issue or complaint, because I would have quickly turned the tables on her. I was an emotional brute, and completely unapproachable. And because of it, there was almost no level of intimacy between us. But now we are both committed to total trust and truth in our relationship, and there are no topics that are off limits. I actually welcome her complaints, because they let me know what I need to do in order to be a better husband.

Healthy marriages are always defined by honesty and openness, especially when it comes to communicating unmet needs and offenses.

"MEN AND WOMEN ARE INHERENTLY DIFFERENT, AND WILL ALMOST ALWAYS SEE ISSUES FROM DIFFERING POINTS OF VIEW."

Principle #3:

Be mindful of your differences. Men and women are inherently different, and will almost always see issues from differing points of view. Men shouldn't expect women to think like men, and vice versa. People also have different personalities and dispositions, and this causes us to see things from unique perspectives. Any time two people have a conflict or problem to work out, you have two distinct points of view to deal with.

Allowing each other the freedom to be different is critical to resolving conflict. You not only have to understand your differences, but must try to see things from the other person's perspective. Trouble comes when we expect our partner to think and feel exactly as we do on an issue. Healthy resolution comes when we acknowledge our differences, and then respect each other's differing points of view.

Principle #4:

Never discuss an issue when you're angry. When resolving conflict, cooler heads always prevail. So never let yourself be sucked into an argument in the heat of anger. The best approach is to simply say, "We really need to work this out, but let's wait until we can both be rational." Then set a time to sit down over coffee and discuss the issue.

This not only gives you both time to cool down, but you can think about what you want to say, and then pray about the situation. If you are being unreasonable, pray that God would reveal that to you. If your partner has offended you, or if you have an unmet need or desire, spend time thinking about the most loving way to bring it up to them. Give yourself time to cool off and prepare for positive confrontation, but don't go to bed angry. Make it a discipline in your marriage to never go to bed in anger, and to always resolve problems quickly.

Principle #5:

Focus on the problem, not each other. Personal attacks or insults are never productive. And passive-aggressive comments are just as bad. When working out conflicts, it is critical to remain focused on the issue, not your partner's perceived faults.

If you feel that your partner has been taking you for granted, give some specific examples of ways in which they have done that. If you feel that they have been spending too much time working or golfing and ignoring your relationship, then calmly and lovingly let them know how that makes you feel.

Let the issue be the issue, not your partner's personal flaws.

Principle #6:

Listen to each other. In the middle of an argument or debate, most of us are so anxious to tell our side of the story that we tend to forget we're there to resolve a problem. It feels good to vent, so that's what we do.

But healthy arguments only happen when two people commit to a give-and-take discussion. We give our point of view, and then truly listen as the other person gives theirs. And listening implies that they might have a very valid point. We should always consider the possibility that our point of view could be wrong.

Principle #7:

Commit to resolving the issue. If at any time during a discussion you feel yourself getting angry or defensive, or if the lines of communication seem to be breaking down, call "Time," and decide to put the discussion on hold until later. Then set a specific time and place to try again.

When a conflict goes unresolved, the temptation is to throw up our hands and let it go, but that's just further avoiding the problem. The goal is to truly resolve the issue so that you can move forward, not allow it to come back and haunt you again in the future.

Principle #8:

Give your problem to God. Always, after talking through an issue, you should pray together, asking God to help you work it out. Ask him to reveal any areas in which you are being blind or unreasonable. Ask him to help you both see each other's points of view. And ask that he use your problem or conflict to draw you closer to each other, instead of farther apart.

Give your problem to God, and then commit to doing whatever he puts on your heart to do, in order to make things right.

An Attitude of Service

There are many other tools and skills needed to successfully resolve marital conflicts, but these are a few of the more critical practices that healthy couples use when working through issues. More important, though, than developing the proper techniques, is having a general attitude of love and respect, as well as a desire to make your marriage all that it can possibly be.

Couples who approach marriage as a lifelong, intimate relationship are willing to put aside their own wants and needs in order to serve the other. And when two people come together with an attitude of service and humility, you have the kind of marriage that God intended all of us to have. The best marriages are always made up of two servants in love.

Resolving conflict is more about a meeting of needs than a meeting of the minds. When it's more important to make your partner happy than to be right, you'll discover a level of peace and intimacy that most couples only dream of.

Develop that kind of servant-attitude now, before you're married, and you'll be miles ahead of the pack whenever struggle comes your way.

CHAPTER ELEVEN

SHARED VISION AND PURPOSE

Whenever I (Jimmy) counsel engaged couples, one of the first questions I ask them is, "Why do you want to get married?"

The answers I get are all over the map, but are almost always some variation of, "Because we're in love," or "Because we want to share our lives together," or "Because we are soul mates."

They usually smile and goo at each other as they answer—which is fine, because that's the way couples are supposed to feel. But I need them to dig deeper, so I ask a few follow-up questions.

"Do you believe God put you together?" I ask.

They always say, "Yes."

"So why do you think he brought you together?"

This is when I usually get blank stares. Most will attempt an answer, but it's obvious they have put very little thought into the idea. It's not that they don't truly believe that God wants them together; they just haven't stopped to wonder why.

What is God's purpose for us as a couple? What does he hope to accomplish through our marriage? Why did he bring us together?

These are the most critical questions any Christian couple can ask, yet very, very few have ever made a serious effort to find out.

Besides counseling engaged couples, I also counsel couples on the brink of divorce. And the first question I ask them is "Why do you want to get divorced?" Unsurprisingly, the answers I get are almost always the exact inverse of why engaged couples say they want to get married.

"Because we're no longer in love." "Because we're tired of sharing our lives together." "Because I didn't marry my soul-mate, and I want to be free to find them."

If "being in love" is your purpose for getting married, what happens when you are no longer feel in love? What happens when you no longer want to share your lives together? What is keeping the marriage alive when you stop feeling like soul mates?

> "FOR MARRIAGE TO LAST, IT HAS TO BE BUILT ON A MUCH GREATER PURPOSE THAN THE HAPPINESS AND WELL-BEING OF TWO SINGLE PEOPLE."

For marriage to last, it has to be built on a much greater purpose than the happiness and well-being of two single people. And that purpose has to be greater than any amount of stress and struggle that comes into the marriage.

When Karen and I got married, we had the best of intentions. And we were sure we were marrying for all the right reasons. We loved each other, and wanted to raise a family together. We wanted to pool our talents and make a good home for our children. We wanted to teach our kids biblical values, and raise them to be good people. But we never put much thought into God's vision for us as a couple.

As a result, a few years into the marriage we found ourselves on the brink of divorce. Our only real purpose seemed to be figuring out how to stay married for the sake of the kids. We were completely out of love, out of infatuation, with no "soul mate" feelings between us. It was an exhausting experience. And neither of us had any idea how to fix the problem.

Becoming One in God's Heart

When God brings couples together, he does so with a great deal of intention and vision. He knows why he created each one of us, and what he wants to accomplish in our lives. He gave us specific gifts and talents in order to fulfill that vision. He knows the plans he has for us, and those plans involve marrying the right person.

God knows exactly who he wants you to marry, and why he wants you to marry them. He knows the children he wants to give you, and has a vision for their future as well. God has a plan and a purpose for each one of us—individually, and as a couple. And it's our job to seek out that vision so that he can fulfill it through us.

Once Karen and I surrendered our marriage to God, he began revealing his purpose for us as a couple. Little by little, we began to see his vision for our marriage, and it completely transformed our relationship. It not only saved our marriage, but gave us renewed energy and purpose. We were once again one in heart, back in love with each other, wanting to share our lives together. We were once again "soul mates," but this time on a much higher level. Our hearts were joined together for a specific vision and purpose. We were working toward God's vision, not our own.

We still had conflict and strife, still had to navigate the inevitable storms of marriage, but those struggles no longer felt insurmountable, because we were working toward a great purpose and vision. We knew that our marriage was ultimately about glorifying God, and God was greater than any problem we could possibly encounter.

We were once again one in heart, but this time we were one in God's heart. And that made all the difference in how we related to each other.

One in God's Purpose

When you become one in God's heart, you become one in God's purpose. And God's purpose is greater than any dream or goal you could envision on your own. Your problems no longer define your marriage; they are simply obstacles of the devil that you need to get past in order to continue with your primary purpose. And you know you can get past them, because God is much bigger than any obstacle the devil can throw at you.

When you are working toward the same purpose, you no longer struggle with those nagging doubts and insecurities that plague so many married couples. Questions like, Did I marry the right person? Are we supposed to stay married? How are we ever going to get through this?

You know that you are exactly where God wants you, married to the person God hand picked for you, because God doesn't make mistakes. You are one in God's purpose, not your own, and God's purpose is greater than your doubts.

When you are one in God's purpose, your marriage is no longer about self-gratification or selfish desires. It's no longer about what your partner can do for you, or what you can get out of the marriage. You don't spend your days sulking because you didn't get your way, or angry because your partner hurt your feelings. You begin to see that God's vision is for you to serve your partner, not yourself, so you focus on their needs, not your own.

God is glorified when married couples serve each other, and when they do that, an amazing thing happens: their own needs and desires are suddenly fulfilled. It is through giving that we begin to receive. It's through self-denial that we find the gratification we need.

When God's purpose becomes our purpose, our relationship takes on an entirely new dimension.

One in God's Will

When you become one in God's heart, you also become one in God's will. And the only way any of us will find true peace and harmony in marriage is to surrender our will to God, and trust him with our future.

When Ruthie and I (Frank) married, one of the greatest struggles we faced was making decisions together as a couple. We were both in our late twenties when we married, and both very strong-willed and opinionated. I had been on my own since the age of eighteen, and was extremely set in my ways. Ruthie was a schoolteacher, and had long since cut loose of her mother's apron strings. We were two very independent-minded people, trying to come together as one, and it wasn't easy for either of us.

I was especially stubborn and uncompromising, and accustomed to getting my way. And I certainly wasn't going to let a little thing like getting married change my way of thinking.

Almost all of our arguments boiled down to a battle of wills. We argued about everything—how to spend our money, which friends we would hang out with, where we would go on vacations, how we would celebrate holidays, even how the house should be decorated. I had opinions on everything, and couldn't understand why Ruthie wouldn't see my way on every subject. The more I tried to control her, the more she pushed back. We were in a constant tug of war.

It was only when we surrendered our stubborn wills to God that we were able to find some form of peace and consensus. I realized that my need to be in control was making our marriage miserable, so I learned to let go and instead work as a team when making decisions.

We had spent so much time butting heads in the early days of our marriage, that we completely lost sight of who should be the true head of our household. So we began submitting our decisions to God.

And the good thing about letting God be the boss of your home is that God is never wrong. He is perfect in every way, and every decision he makes is flawless. When God is in charge, everyone wins.

Submitting to God's will is never easy, and we still struggle every day to let go. But it has proven to bring more peace and contentment to our marriage than any decision we've ever made.

At the root of every struggling marriage is a monumental battle of wills. And the most dysfunctional families are always those where parents are fighting each other for control.

Becoming one in God's heart begins by submitting to God's will. It not only transforms your marriage, but transfers the burden of decision-making onto God's shoulders. And that's exactly where it belongs.

One In God's Love

When you become one in God's heart, you also become one in God's love. And God's love is different than our love.

Our love is fleeting and fickle. It is based more on emotion than determination. It is almost always conditional and undependable, and can change as often as the tides.

But God's love is steady and relentless. It is unchanging and unconditional. It is the same yesterday, today, and tomorrow. God's love is agape love, the kind of love that says, "I'm going to stay true to you until the end of time, no matter what you do, no matter how I feel, no matter how strained our relationship becomes. I will never leave you nor forsake you. You are mine, and I am yours, and our relationship is an eternal one."

God's love is a non-negotiable love. A love that is fully committed, fully invested in the relationship, fully devoted to the other's best interest. It is unwavering and faithful and true.

And when you and I become one in God's heart, he transfers his power to love onto us. When we surrender to God's purpose, and submit to God's will, he imparts within us the fruits of his love.

Paul tells us, "But the fruit of the Spirit is love, joy, peace, forbearance, kindness, goodness, faithfulness, gentleness and self-control."

Imagine a marriage between two people who always displayed those godly characteristics. Two people who were always loving and joyful toward each other. Who were always peaceful in the midst of stress, and forbearing in times of trouble. Who always acted kind toward each other, even when they didn't feel like it. Who were good and faithful and gentle in every circumstance. People who displayed self-control in the midst of conflict.

Do you think they would have a good marriage? Wouldn't you love to have that kind of marriage?

Through the power of the Holy Spirit, we all have the ability to operate in God's love—in agape love. He promises to fill us with his Spirit if we ask. And when God's Spirit fills us, his love flows through us.

Finding God's Vision

Karen and I live and move as one. We are one in heart, because we are one in purpose. We operate in God's vision, and everything we do and say is connected to that vision. God is fulfilling his purpose through us, and God's purpose is what keeps our love alive. It is literally the reason we get up in the morning, and the one thing that keeps our marriage infused with passion.

Every healthy marriage is built on a shared vision and purpose. And if that vision isn't God's vision, it isn't worth working toward. If your vision is for money or fame or education or achievement or any other human endeavor, I guarantee it won't last. And it won't bring you the happiness you hope for. Earthly visions are as fleeting as they are meaningless.

But God's visions are significant and eternal. They are the only goals worth setting, and the only purposes that will keep your marriage together.

If you've found yourself heading toward marriage, but haven't asked yourself why you're getting married, it's important to take time to do that. Talk to your fiancé about the purpose of your marriage. Why do you think God brought us together? What does he hope to accomplish through our marriage? What is his vision and purpose for us as a couple?

If you don't know, spend time in prayer and fasting in order to find out.

If the person you're dating is the one God wants you to marry, God also has a vision for your future as a couple. And he is eager to reveal that vision to you. Don't get so busy planning a wedding that you miss it.

* * * * * *

At MarriageToday, we have a special resource called The Mountaintop of Marriage. It is a guide to help couples plan their own "Vision Retreat," which is something we suggest every married couple do at least once a year. This resource walks couples through the process of developing a clear and common purpose for their marriage, and can also be a great tool for engaged couples as they prepare for marriage.

You can order it on our website at *www.marriagetoday.com.*

CHAPTER
TWELVE

PHYSICAL AND SPIRITUAL INTIMACY

I (Jimmy) have made a living making mistakes in my marriage and then talking about them from the pulpit. So far I've never run out of good sermon material.

There was a time in my life when I would have never been able to admit my failures, but God cured me of that long ago. In the early years of our marriage I was an emotional brute, and I could never let Karen have the upper hand in an argument. I ruled our home with an iron fist. In reality I was deeply fearful and insecure, but I put on a good front.

We had absolutely no intimacy in our marriage during those days, and we were both miserable. It is exhausting to think back on how painfully unhappy we were. God stepped in and miraculously healed our marriage, and it all began the first time I admitted to Karen that I was wrong. That moment is burned into my memory, because it was a pivotal point in our relationship.

It happened about three years into our marriage. I was sitting in the living room of our home, fuming over another bitter argument we'd had, and I could hear Karen crying and packing her bags in the back bedroom. Moments earlier I had screamed at the top of my lungs for her to pack her bags and leave, but I didn't really think she would do it. We'd had blowout fights before, too many times to count, and it wasn't the first time I had lost my temper. But somehow I knew that this time I had gone too far.

As I sat fuming, listening to her cries of sorrow from the other room, I realized that I was about to lose Karen for good, and the thought chilled me to the core.

"TRYING TO BUILD A HEALTHY MARRIAGE WITHOUT INTIMACY IS LIKE TRYING TO START A CAR WITHOUT A BATTERY. INTIMACY IS WHAT MAKES THE MARRIAGE WORK."

I'm still not sure where I found the courage, but I swallowed my pride, walked into the bedroom and told Karen I was sorry. She immediately softened, and the two of us embraced. It was the most tender moment we'd had in as long as I could remember.

God used that moment of brokenness and honesty as the first step in healing our marriage. I still had a lot to learn about being a decent husband, but from that moment forward he began teaching me the beauty of openness and humility.

Today we have a level of trust and intimacy that I never dreamed we could develop. We have no secrets between us, no hidden needs or agendas, no resentments, no simmering anger, absolutely no walls or barriers keeping us apart. I can tell Karen anything, and she can do the same with me.

I've become addicted to intimacy. I love the closeness and openness that Karen and I share in our relationship, and I would never again do anything to jeopardize it. I would never allow our marriage to go back to the way things once were.

Four Traits of Intimacy

Trying to build a healthy marriage without intimacy is like trying to start a car without a battery. Intimacy is what makes the marriage work. It is the spark that keeps your love alive and keeps the marriage running. Without it, you have nothing but a dead charge and a lot of frustration.

And intimacy can do more than heal your marriage; it can also heal your body. It can cure depression, rebuild low self-esteem, and renew your sense of self worth. It has been proven that people in happy marriages actually have a longer life expectancy because they have better mental and physical health. They recover faster from illnesses, and are much less likely to suffer from emotional disorders.

Intimacy also makes you much better looking to each other. I'm living proof of that, because after over forty years of marriage I'm still married to the most beautiful woman in the world.

But intimacy doesn't happen by accident. It takes hard work, discipline, and intentionality. You have to determine that intimacy is what you most want in your relationship, and then set out to do whatever it takes to build it.

Though there are a lot of different traits and practices needed to develop intimacy in marriage, I've discovered four primary dynamics that must be present in order for it to happen. These four ingredients are value, energy, sacrifice, and openness.

Value

There is a natural progression that happens in almost every marriage. While dating, couples are focused entirely on each other. The relationship is fresh and new and exciting, and they put all their energies into making each moment fun and memorable. They value the relationship, and because of it, their hearts become bound together.

This continues for months after the wedding, because they are still so excited about the new future they are building together. But then as life progresses, the newness of marriage begins to wear a bit thin. They start settling into the relationship, and slowly begin taking each other for granted. The busyness of work and bills start to feel monotonous, and navigating life together often brings tension and conflict. The enthusiasm they once had slowly begins to fade.

Then come kids and even more bills and more conflict, and before they know it, they find themselves focusing on everything but each other. The relationship takes a back seat to the urgencies of life.

This is a common and predictable progression, but it can easily destroy a relationship if left to run its course. For marriage to work, couples need to keep each other at the top of their priority list. The only thing more important than your relationship to each other is your respective relationships to God. All other things must take a back seat to the marriage.

My friends all know that I value their friendship greatly, but not more than I value my relationship with Karen. I love my church family, and will always be there to pastor them through any crisis, but I will never put their needs above Karen's needs. Even my children understand that though I love them more than life itself, my marriage will always come first. There is no earthly relationship that takes a higher spot on my list of priorities than my relationship with Karen.

What you value in life, you bring strength to. You breathe life into it. You nourish and protect and cultivate it. What you value becomes your primary focus and motivation. And when you value your mate above all other earthly things and relationships, the reward is unencumbered intimacy.

When couples come to me for counseling because their marriage isn't working, this is the first thing I help them change. I encourage them to stop putting their focus on work and bills and kids and instead re-focus on each other. I tell them that if they want their marriage to be the way it was when they first married, they have to begin seeing each other the way they did when they first fell in love.

When love fades, it is always because intimacy has taken a back seat to less important matters. And the first step to rebuilding intimacy is re-prioritizing your world and putting marriage back on the top pedestal, where it belongs.

God first. Marriage second. Everything else comes next.

Energy

When God created Eve for Adam, he said, "Therefore shall a man leave his father and his mother, and shall cleave unto his wife: and they shall be one flesh."

The ancient Hebrew word used for cleave in this passage is a dynamic and energetic word. It's a word that implies struggle and effort, like you would use climbing a mountain. There is nothing idle or passive about it. Cleaving takes work and determination.

There is a deep misconception today among many people that marriage should be effortless and natural. I can't count how many people have sat in my office during counseling and said, "Marriage just shouldn't be this hard. It shouldn't be this much of a struggle."

People believe that if they had only married their soul mate, love would naturally fall into place and life would be easy and uncomplicated. They somehow think that if they have to work at the relationship, then maybe it isn't meant to be.

That idea is a lie from the devil, and it couldn't be further from the truth.

Imagine an accomplished composer sitting at his desk, about to begin work on a new composition, and suddenly throwing up his hands and saying, "I give up. Composing music shouldn't be this hard. If this arrangement were meant to be written, it would just come naturally!"

> "THERE IS A DEEP MISCONCEPTION TODAY AMONG MANY PEOPLE THAT MARRIAGE SHOULD BE EFFORTLESS AND NATURAL."

We'd all laugh, because we know instinctively that composing is hard work. It takes a massive amount of time and energy, no matter how talented you happen to be. There is nothing easy or effortless about it.

I (Frank) have been writing for over twenty years, and I've yet to learn how to "crank out" a book. It takes a staggering amount of work and research and time to produce a manuscript worthy of publication. Imagine if I said to an editor, "This book just isn't working. Writing shouldn't be this hard. If books were meant to be written, they would come much more naturally."

If I did that, my last book would be my last book, because you don't sign on to write unless you're willing to put the time and effort into seeing it through.

Nothing worthwhile in life comes easily. It takes energy to make marriage work, and effort to grow an intimate relationship. It doesn't come naturally to anyone, no matter how perfectly suited you are for marriage.

If you married the perfect mate, you would still have to work at the relationship. And you would still have to put time and effort into building an intimate marriage.

The good news is, the rewards of intimacy far outweigh any amount of effort you have to put into it. And the harder you work, the greater intimacy you can build.

Sacrifice

Selfishness is the greatest sin you can commit against your marriage. Selfishness says, I don't want to sacrifice for this relationship. I want this marriage to be about my needs and desires. I don't want to serve; I want to be served."

Selfishness is demanding to get your way instead of looking to the needs of others. And in marriage, it is the worst possible attitude you could have. The only way two people can become one flesh is through sacrifice and self-denial.

I (Jimmy) have always loved golf, and early in our marriage I was at the top of my game. I golfed with friends several afternoons a week, and almost every Saturday. It was a tremendous source of fun and relief for me. But Karen became deeply resentful of my golfing because of the time it took away from her and the kids. My love of golf became the source of many of our arguments.

For a long time, I thought it was wrong of Karen to complain, since golf gave me so much satisfaction. But one day, while praying, God spoke to my spirit in a powerful way. He told me to give up golf. I argued with him, but his conviction was very clear. I knew I needed to obey, so I hung my clubs in the garage and went cold turkey. I gave up golf and instead began coming straight home from work every day to spend time with Karen.

That was a tough sacrifice for me, because I really love golf, but the dividends of that decision paid out ten-fold over the coming years. The fact that I was willing to give up my favorite activity for the sake of my family spoke volumes to Karen about how much our relationship meant to me.

And her response was like nothing I could have imagined. You would have thought I had walked on water while holding back a hurricane with my bare hands. Karen became more loving and tender and attentive—and yes, guys, more sexually responsive—than she had ever been. My willingness to give up golf for my family was a greater boost to our marriage than anything I had ever done. I began wondering what else I could give up.

When the kids got older, Karen encouraged me to take up golf again, and the Lord released me to do so, but I have never allowed it to become the priority that it once was.

I (Frank) have always loved riding motorcycles, and used to ride often before I was married. But Ruthie was always afraid that I would get hurt. While we were dating, she let me know how much she worried every time I would go for a ride. I always thought her fear was irrational, but I'm sure that it didn't feel that way to her.

When we began talking about marriage, she told me that her greatest fear was that I would be hurt or killed in a motorcycle accident and leave her a widow at a young age, even though I was always a very careful rider.

I decided that Ruthie was more important to me than riding, so I sold my prized motorcycle in order to buy her an engagement ring. It was perhaps the greatest sacrifice I could have made at the time, and she instinctively knew that. I was stunned by how much that sacrificial act meant to her.

I promised her at the time that as long as we had children in the house I would never ride motorcycles, and I remained true to that promise. Then a few years ago, on my fiftieth birthday, she encouraged me to buy another motorcycle as her present to me. Our kids were already grown, and both in love with Jesus, so their eternal fate was sealed. And she wanted to honor my sacrifice by making a sacrifice of her own.

Today she's still afraid of motorcycles, but often encourages me to go riding on the weekends, simply because she knows how much I enjoy it. And from time to time, she even agrees to ride with me, as long as I stay on side roads and ride slowly.

Giving up motorcycles for the sake of Ruthie's peace of mind was a small sacrifice, but it meant more to her than anything I could have done.

Sacrifice is the meat and potatoes of marriage. It is where talk turns to action. You don't serve someone by simply thinking about it. You get out of your chair and grab the serving platter. Sacrifice is doing the things that your spouse needs from you, both physically and emotionally. And doing them with an attitude of joy, humility, and self-denial.

In marriage, your partner needs to see that you mean what you say, not in theory, but in practice. And when you do that, you develop a level of spiritual and physical intimacy that most couples can only dream of.

Men, do you want more physical intimacy in your marriage? Then get up and do the dishes. Take the trash out before she even has to ask. Hold her purse while she shops for clothes. Offer to take care of the kids on Saturday so she can hang out with her girlfriends. Look for ways to serve her, and just see how romantic she suddenly becomes.

Women, do you want your husband to be more intimate? Then fight the urge to nag him when he forgets to clean out the garage. Make him his favorite dinner when you know he's had a hard day. Tell him all the ways you admire him, even when he messes up. And from time to time, dig out that little cheerleader outfit, just to let him know you still think he's a hunk.

Sacrifice is doing what makes your partner happy, simply because you care. And it is guaranteed to bring greater intimacy to your marriage.

Openness

When I (Jimmy) speak, people often comment on my willingness to be transparent. I often share very embarrassing and intimate things about our marriage and my past failures, and people are surprised that I'm willing to admit what an idiot I have been. I honestly don't even think about it that much, because openness has become so second nature to me. Today I am an open book, because God has burned every ounce of arrogance and pride from my spirit. I have nothing to hide—from Karen, or anyone else.

Because of the pain I experienced in childhood, I carried a lot of anger and resentment into adulthood, and it was devastating to our marriage. God healed my wounded spirit and taught me the power of openness and honesty—not just in my marriage, but in every area of life. I'm willing to share my failures, because God uses them to help heal other broken marriages. And also because it has done so much to bring healing and intimacy to our marriage.

Karen and I are closer than we've ever been, because we keep no secrets from each other. She is my safe place, and I am hers. We can tell each other anything, with no fear of judgment or retribution.

Our inner thoughts and feelings are our holy of holies. They are the most helpless and defenseless part of our being. All of our doubts and insecurities are hidden deep inside in order to keep us from getting hurt. When we open up to another person, we are exposing the most vulnerable parts of ourselves. And in doing so, we risk being wounded or betrayed.

But true spiritual intimacy demands that we take that risk. It's impossible to build a truly close relationship with someone when you are hiding secrets.

Intimacy demands complete trust, openness, and vulnerability. These things are bellwether traits of every truly great marriage.

CHAPTER THIRTEEN

A SPIRIT OF COMPATIBILITY

On paper, Ruthie and I (Frank) appear to be certifiably incompatible. We have more differences between us than similarities. We realized this fact within the first few months of our marriage, but it first became apparent just two days into our honeymoon.

I had booked a beautiful room in the nicest hotel I could afford for the first night of our honeymoon, and we had a wonderful evening together. But the next morning I woke up around eight to an empty bed. Ruthie was nowhere in sight, and I couldn't imagine where she had gone. I wondered if she might have come to her senses in the night and hitched a ride home to her mother's.

I got dressed and wandered the halls of the hotel looking for her. I eventually found her sitting alone in the hotel dining room, her eyes red and swollen from crying. She had already finished her breakfast, and didn't even look up when I sat down across from her.

"What's wrong?" I asked. She immediately burst into tears.

"You're sorry you married me, aren't you?" she cried out, her head buried deep in her hands.

"Of course I'm not," I protested, wondering why she would think such a thing. No matter how hard I tried to convince her otherwise, she seemed convinced that I was somehow in a state of remorse.

We talked for nearly an hour before I finally discovered the reason for her tears. Apparently, Ruthie was a morning person who popped out of bed every day at the crack of dawn. The only days she allowed herself to sleep late were when she was either sick or depressed.

I, on the other hand, am a card-carrying night owl. I function better at night, and love it when I can sleep late in the mornings. Alarm clocks are the bane of my existence.

This was something we had never discussed before getting married, so when I didn't wake up bright and early the first morning of our marriage, Ruthie just assumed I was depressed. And obviously, she was the reason for my depression.

I know. It still doesn't make sense, but that was our first morning together.

Ruthie was also exhausted from lack of sleep, and that's another reason she was crying. I never thought to tell her that I snored like a freight train, and jostled wildly in my sleep. Ruthie, on the other hand, is an incredibly light sleeper.

You'd have thought that would have come up before the wedding.

Creating Compatibility

Over the coming months, we discovered a host of other ways in which we appeared to be completely incompatible. I am a spender who hates living on a budget; she is a saver, incredibly frugal and thrifty. I'm an extrovert who loves parties; Ruthie would rather sit home by the fire. I love taking risks; she's careful and cautious. I'm a people pleaser who has never met a stranger; she's more reserved and pragmatic and picks her friends carefully.

On almost every level, we are very different. Yet we've been able to build a strong and successful marriage. In fact, today we are best friends, and madly in love with each other. And our love continues to grow stronger with each passing year! In spite of our conflicting qualities and natures, in spite of being different in so many ways, we have developed a strong and healthy marriage.

And that didn't happen by accident. The differences we faced were very real issues, not petty disagreements that would work themselves out if we looked the other way. It took a lot of patience and compromise and self-sacrifice to work things though. We had to learn to become compatible, because it certainly wasn't something that came naturally to us as a couple.

Compatibility is not something we had; it's something we created. It was a process of growing in love in spite of our differing traits and personalities. It was a decision to not only accept each other's conflicting outlooks and qualities, but to embrace them as the defining feature that made our marriage fun and unique.

Nobody really marries the exact right person. And no couples are completely compatible from day one. You become right for each other through hard work and patience and a spirit of self-sacrifice. Through developing an attitude of giving instead of demanding. Through learning to compromise, even though you feel like digging in your heels. Through choosing to serve instead of wanting to be served.

> **"COMPATIBILITY IS NOT SOMETHING WE HAD; IT'S SOMETHING WE CREATED."**

You don't just marry the right person. You must become the right person. And they in turn set out to become the right person for you.

Why Compatibility is Important

Having said all of that, there is still a very good reason that pastors and counselors conduct compatibility assessments during pre-marital counseling. Because engaged couples need to go into marriage with their eyes wide open.

I (Jimmy) have been counseling engaged couples for over thirty years, and I always begin by assessing the couple's level of compatibility. I've developed a series of tests and questionnaires to help me do that. It's my job to uncover any areas of potential trouble or conflict, and I take that role seriously. If I see any relational red flags or character flaws, it would be wrong of me not to bring those issues to the surface. And areas of incompatibility are high on my list of red flags to watch for.

The struggles that Frank and Ruthie experienced during the early years of their marriage were difficult, but they were not insurmountable. Their differing viewpoints and personalities were tough hurdles to overcome, but they were not impossible.

Karen and I had many of those same struggles during the early years of our marriage, and it took a lot of hard work and compromise to bridge the differences between us. Still today, we have very different traits and personalities, yet we've learned to become compatible. Because of it, we've been able to grow a marriage that is not only successful, but infinitely happy and rewarding.

In my years as a pastor and counselor I've learned that couples can overcome any problem or obstacle with the right attitude and desire.

Jesus tells us, "With God all things are possible," and nowhere is this more true than in the context of marriage. Any couple who leans on God for help and understanding can make their marriage work, no matter how diverse or incompatible they appear to be.

There are no issues of incompatibility in marriage that can't be overcome. That is a promise from God, and a reality I've seen time and again in my years of ministry.

All that having been said, there are areas of differences that make compatibility extremely difficult. And those are the areas of potential conflict that couples need to identify and address before standing at the altar.

Five Areas of Potential Conflict

As a counselor, it's not my role to point out all the ways a couple is likely to be compatible. It would be a lot more fun to simply pat them on the back, encourage them to focus on the positive, and just ignore the rest, but that would be a monumental injustice to them.

My job is to point out areas of potential incompatibility—issues that are likely to cause stress and turmoil. I'm there to identify differences in attitude and character and mindset that are likely to bring a great deal of trouble and divergence as they attempt to navigate their future life together. I try to be encouraging, but also realistic.

Though there are a number of areas and issues that can make marriage a major challenge, there are five key differences in background and mindset that I tend to watch for. Though I don't consider any of these areas of divergence deal-breakers, they do give me cause for pause.

These five areas of potential conflict have one thing in common: they all have a foundational impact on the way we think, feel, and process information. And each of these areas can easily create a seemingly insurmountable level of conflict and incompatibility.

These five key areas are: culture, parity, emotional health, character, and values.

Culture

The world is growing smaller by the day, and because of it, more and more couples from different cultures and backgrounds are getting married. Many of these couples grow up with vastly different experiences and upbringings. This isn't necessarily an insurmountable issue, but it can create a unique set of challenges and frustrations.

When couples come from different countries or regions, they have likely grown up with unique traditions and holidays, and they have to decide which of these they will celebrate with their children. One partner will probably have to live far away from their parents and other relatives, and one set of grandparents will almost certainly feel slighted. There are language barriers to deal with, and kids may not get to know all of their cousins. You may also struggle to understand each other's humor, and having to explain your jokes can get very old.

The biggest hurdle, though, is that people from different countries and cultures tend to simply think differently. They tend to have different values and mindsets and outlooks.

I (Frank) know a young man who was engaged to a beautiful young girl from Eastern Europe. They were both Christians, and had a strong mutual attraction, but their differences in culture weighed on their relationship. While they were dating, these differences seemed fun and exciting, and actually made their relationship feel more interesting. But once they began talking about marriage, their different worldviews became a constant source of struggle.

Every small issue turned into a battle of cultures between them, and they began arguing over even the smallest decisions. Eventually they decided to break off the relationship. It was sad to see them part ways, but they likely saved themselves from a lot of future pain and heartache, had they decided to get married.

Interracial marriages can bring an even greater number of challenges. I would never encourage an interracial couple to break off an engagement because of skin colors or cultures, but I do make a point of warning them of the unique struggles they are likely to face.

Many of the challenges faced by interracial couples come from outside the marriage, often from their own families. Prejudices run deep in certain areas of the world, so they are likely to face open hostility and intimidation from others. They will be stereotyped, and may have to deal with insults, slights, and whispers from strangers.

Raising children of mixed identities can also prove difficult—for both the parents and the kids. They, too, will likely struggle with unwarranted stereotypes and prejudices.

On top of all this, interracial couples often have to navigate their differing cultures and traditions, and find a way to celebrate them that will feel meaningful to both partners.

Racial and cultural differences don't cause marriages to fail, and like all challenges in marriage, they can be overcome. But often it takes a great deal of creativity, compromise and understanding from all parties to do so. Couples need to be prepared for a lot of purposeful dialogue and agreement, and an even greater level of patience and compassion if they want their marriage to work.

Physical and Social Parity

There are times when couples come to me (Jimmy) for counseling and on the surface they appear to be a good match. They have a lot of similar tastes and interests, and both come from Christian families. There isn't a glaring red flag in their relationship that I see. But the further I dig, the more I realize how different they are in backgrounds and experiences.

She may have grown up in a wealthy family, and be accustomed to a very comfortable lifestyle. She's used to traveling to exotic locations, dining in the finest restaurants, and rubbing elbows with the rich and powerful. Her family has never had to worry about money, so she has never had to live on a budget.

He, on the other hand, might have come from a blue-collar home, where money was always tight. He's never been out of the country, and wouldn't know which fork to use at a fancy dinner. He's a pleasant enough fellow, and carries himself well, so she doesn't see his lack of money as a problem. But the two grew up in very different worlds.

This type of rich-meets-poor disparity among couples may play out well in fairy tales, but in real life, it can lead to a great deal of conflict. He will never be able to provide the lifestyle to which she is accustomed, and will likely always feel a bit inadequate and intimidated around her parents. And she will always struggle to fit in with his family and friends.

Social status is just one area of disparity that can lead to conflict.

While living in Texas, I (Frank) had a friend who was a body builder, and at the time training to compete in the Mr. Texas Bodybuilding Championship. He was serious about his sport, and would often spend six to eight hours a day in the gym. He was always on a very regimented diet.

I was stunned one day to learn that he was dating a girl who had never once been to the gym. She was addicted to fast food, and never quite understood his fascination with health and fitness. Their attraction was always a mystery to me, and I knew they were heading toward trouble.

The two decided to get married, and within a few months of the wedding she began putting on weight. She had gained over fifty pounds by their first anniversary. He told me once how much this bothered him, and I encouraged him to get into joint counseling, but I don't believe that he ever did. The couple eventually divorced.

Marriage is difficult under even the best of circumstances. But when you come into marriage with vastly different socioeconomic experiences and backgrounds, or with possible differences in interests, beliefs, intelligence, and education, those difficulties are only compounded.

Couples almost always believe that these disparities won't matter, but they always have an impact. It's easy to fall for someone from a completely different world, and there's no reason those marriages can't last, but couples need to be realistic about the inevitable difficulties they will face.

Emotional Health

We've all heard the old adage "opposites attract," and we see it play out in a lot of marriages. A shy and mousy girl will gravitate toward a loud and boisterous man. A young man who never says two words in conversation will marry a woman who can't seem to stop talking.

In some cases this is a natural inclination that most of us have. In relationships, we gravitate toward people with traits that we wish we had. On a subconscious level we are looking for someone to "complete" us, so we're naturally attracted to people with personality traits that we lack.

But often there is a much different dynamic at work. In many cases, it is our dysfunctions and insecurities that are doing the gravitating. When you see a dominant and controlling woman married to a passive and submissive man, you're witnessing two wounded and unhealthy people who have been drawn together by a strange sense of co-dependence.

> "WE'VE ALL HEARD THE OLD ADAGE "OPPOSITES ATTRACT," AND WE SEE IT PLAY OUT IN A LOT OF MARRIAGES."

People always marry to the level of their emotional health. Emotionally wounded people naturally gravitate toward other emotionally wounded people. It is textbook co-dependent behavior, and it never makes for a happy marriage relationship.

When I (Jimmy) see this dynamic at work during pre-marital counseling, I become brutally honest with both partners, and almost always encourage them to put the wedding on hold until they can work through their individual issues. It takes two healthy and happy people to create a healthy, happy marriage. It doesn't work any other way.

Character

I'm not sure I've ever quoted Bill Murray, but I read something he said in a recent interview that really caught my attention. He was talking about people who were considering getting married and his advice to them was this:

"Buy a plane ticket for the two of you to travel all around the world, and go to places that are hard to go to and hard to get out of. And if... when you land in

JFK… you're still in love with that person, get married at the airport."

I'm sure he was just being funny, but his advice wasn't that far off base. I actually think he has a good point, although I obviously don't believe couples should travel together in an intimate manner before marriage.

Before you marry someone, you need to know their true inner character, and the best way to do that is to see them in all kinds of settings and situations. You need to know how they handle stress, how they react when they're angry, how they deal with grief and loss and disappointment, how they respond to conflict and disagreements, how they act and react during moments of intense pressure. When we are squeezed and pressed, our true character is exposed. And that's something you need to see before standing at the altar, not after.

This is one reason I'm in favor of long dating relationships, because it allows couples to spend time together in all types of situations. They can see how the other behaves around friends, family, co-workers, waiters, bosses, and anyone else they come into contact with.

People of strong moral character make exceptional marriage partners. But people who tell white lies, who tend to be dishonest and deceitful, who cheat or steal or gossip, who show a basic lack of good character, will only grow worse after the wedding.

Values

During my (Jimmy's) many years of counseling, the thing that always surprised me most was the number of couples who had never taken time to talk about their dreams and visions for the future. They're planning to spend the rest of their lives together, yet they haven't made an effort to discuss what is most important to them, what drives them, what motivates them, where they want life to take them, where they hope to be ten, twenty, and thirty years in the future. They haven't discussed their dreams for their family, their career, or their expectations for marriage.

The things we value and cherish in life say more about us than any words we could utter. Our goals and dreams are what make us unique from every other person. So how can you successfully build a life with another person without first knowing that you share the same basic dreams and values?

Too many couples go into marriage with conflicting goals and expectations, and they don't even know it until they've already exchanged rings. Suddenly they are navigating life together and realize they are going in different directions. And their differing values become a huge source of conflict.

Shared values and expectations are at the heart of what makes marriage work. There are far too many daily decisions to be made that hinge directly on the family's shared vision and goals. If you don't have a shared destination and mindset, you will find yourself in constant battle.

If you haven't discussed your life-values with your potential spouse, it's time to begin.

A Spirit of Compatibility

There is no such thing as a perfectly matched couple, because no two people are truly alike.

By our very natures, men and women are different. No matter how many things we think we have in common, we will always find areas of disagreement and conflict, because we are simply wired differently by design.

We also live in a fallen world, filled with sinful and wounded people, and that creates a breeding ground for conflict. Anytime you have a marriage, you have two flawed and damaged people deciding to navigate life together in the same space and circumstance. A perfectly compatible couple doesn't exist because there is no such thing as two perfect people.

The word "compatible" is derived from the words "compassion" and "able." And it is defined as, "capable of existing or living together in harmony." It is the ability to live in compassion with another person. It doesn't mean that you become perfectly in sync, or that you always agree, just that you are capable of overlooking those areas of disagreement and living in harmony in spite of them.

When I (Jimmy) counsel couples, I set out to gauge their level of compatibility, but what I'm really looking for is a spirit of compatibility. I'm looking for a basic willingness and ability to become compatible. I want to see couples who have a strong desire to overcome the differences between them and create a workable level of compatibility within the relationship.

Compatibility is not innate in any of us; it is earned. You become compatible through compromise and negotiation, and by making a commitment to the relationship. It is a process, a disposition, and a willingness to work together to bridge any areas of conflict or divergence.

That's true for couples who have everything in common, and for couples who have almost nothing in common.

Marriage is about overcoming trials and obstacles, and any two people who commit to working together can make a marriage work.

But only you can tell if marriage to a certain person is the right step to take. Determining compatibility ultimately falls to you and your partner. And that is what the next section of this book is designed to help you do.

Time to Talk About Marriage

For those readers who are either engaged or in the courting phase of your relationship, the following section of this book is designed specifically for you. It is intended as a tool for assessing the strength (or weakness) of your relationship, as well as your preparedness for marriage.

If you haven't made a regular habit of having open and honest conversations with your potential mate about your future, this is the time to begin. And you'll find all the tools and direction you need to do so on the coming pages.

This next section is designed as a way to get you and your partner talking about your future, and discussing topics that are critical to your relationship. If you haven't had open and frank dialogue about the principles and expectations of marriage, then here is your opportunity.

The best approach might be for the two of you to read through this section together and then discuss each question as it comes. And don't rush through it. Take every rabbit trail you find along the way, because you may run across an important issue that needs to be addressed.

Many of these questions have no right or wrong answer, but are instead matters of logistics or expectations. How many kids should you have? Who should handle the money? Where should you spend the holidays? These are things that every couple has to work out on their own, and the best time to work them out is now, before you find yourself in the heat of an argument.

Other questions do have a right and wrong answer in the eyes of God, and in those cases we've elaborated on them further. As a pastor, it's my job to teach what the Bible says, and I've never shied away from speaking the truth.

This next section is not a substitute for pre-marital counseling, but it's a great way to get the juices of communication flowing.

SECTION THREE

Let's Talk
About Marriage

CHAPTER FOURTEEN

LET'S TALK ABOUT ROLES

I (Frank) find it a little embarrassing to admit this, but as a child I did very little housework. It just wasn't expected of me, and I can't remember ever complaining about it.

I do remember helping to clear the table after big meals from time to time, but that usually involved taking my plate to the sink and then slipping away to play in the back yard with my brothers. My mom did almost all the housework, including making our beds each morning after we left for school.

Mom grew up on a farm in Germany, with fourteen brothers and sisters, and in those days the chores were very clearly delegated. The girls took care of the home while the men worked the field. At harvest time, the whole family would come together to get the crops into the barn, but during the rest of the year they all kept their roles clearly defined. It worked because everyone had a job, and they all knew what they were supposed to do.

I didn't grow up on a farm, but Mom was still in the habit of doing most of the housework. I'm not sure how my sister Angela drew the short straw, but she was always expected to help.

I still remember the first time that fact came up in conversation with Ruthie, just a few months into our marriage.

"You didn't make your bed growing up?" she said, her mouth wide open. Somehow it never sounded bad until she said it aloud. And in that tone.

"Well, I wouldn't say never," I said sheepishly.

I'm thinking, Maybe I should have found a better time to bring that up?

She's thinking, Buddy, I'm not your mom, and I say it's about time you learned how!

Needless to say, Ruthie and I had a lot of details to work out when it came to role expectations in the home.

Defining Your Roles

Clearly-defined roles and expectations are critical to keeping peace in a relationship. They not only keep the home running, they alleviate confusion and resentment between married couples.

Roles serve two purposes in marriage.

First, they serve to fulfill each partner's basic needs. Though it's true that no two people are alike, and we all have our own unique traits and personalities, men and women are hard wired with distinctly different needs within a marriage. And though these needs differ in importance from person to person, I've found them to be universal to every relationship between men and women.

> "CLEARLY-DEFINED ROLES AND EXPECTATIONS ARE CRITICAL TO KEEPING PEACE IN A RELATIONSHIP. THEY NOT ONLY KEEP THE HOME RUNNING, THEY ALLEVIATE CONFUSION AND RESENTMENT BETWEEN MARRIED COUPLES."

The four primary needs of women are: security, open and honest communication, non-sexual touch and affection, and leadership.

And the four primary needs of men are: honor, friendship, sex, and domestic support.

I (Jimmy) have counseled married couples for over thirty years, and I have yet to see a relationship where this didn't hold true. Men and women are designed by God with very different physical and emotional needs, and the roles we perform in marriage must serve to fulfill these differing needs.

Second, clearly defined roles help fulfill the basic functions of marriage. In real terms, they make sure that the daily tasks of running a home get covered. Falling in love is often filled with unicorns and rainbows, but being married means someone has to mow the lawn and do the laundry.

Roles are like the pistons of the marital engine. In order for the relationship to run smoothly, all the pistons have to fire in sync.

And the functional roles you play are adaptable to your own specific gifts and personalities. In a traditional marriage, the husband often works outside the home while the wife takes care of the children, then they each have specific chores in order to keep the house running smoothly. Maybe the husband will do the lawn work and keep the garage clean, while the wife takes care of the housework.

Feminists may balk at this stereotype, but that's how men and women have traditionally defined their roles—at least in past generations. But these are not hard and fast rules, and today things are very different. I know couples who have completely reversed roles in their relationship and it works well for them.

In some homes, the wife may decide to work outside the home and the husband might stay home and take care of the children. Maybe the wife is better at yard work, and the husband enjoys vacuuming. It doesn't matter what you do, or how your roles are defined, only that you take time to clearly define them. Otherwise you may find yourself arguing over menial tasks, like who is supposed to take out the garbage, how the plants will get watered, and who keeps the house stocked with groceries.

Often during pre-marital counseling, I will ask these types of specific questions and the couples learn for the first time that they have completely differing expectations regarding their roles in the home. They will discuss it and come to a workable compromise. Five minutes of discussion has likely saved them from five years of arguing, simply because they took the time to talk it through and come up with a workable solution.

Here then are some of the more specific questions you should be discussing regarding your roles in the relationship:

In your paradigm, what is the husband's role in the home? And what is the wife's role?

Most of us come into marriage with very specific ideas about who should do what within the marriage. And these ideas were usually formed by our own experiences in childhood. Talk about how you imagine that things will be in your home, and how your potential mate feels about these things. See how similar—or different—your ideas might be.

How did you arrive at your specific views and ideas in this area?

Most of us have developed our role concepts by watching our parents. If you grew up in a traditional home, where the father worked and the mother cared for the children, that will likely be your expectation in marriage. If your mother worked outside the home, you may likely expect to work as well. Talk about your experiences as a child, and how that has shaped your view of roles in the home. It always helps to understand why we think the way we do when negotiating our future roles in the home.

Do you believe the husband should be the head of the household? If so, what does that mean to you?

Paul wrote to the church at Ephesus, "Submit to one another out of reverence for Christ. Wives, submit to your husbands as to the Lord. For the husband is the head of the wife as Christ is the head of the church... Husbands, love your wives, just as Christ loved the church and gave himself up for her."

Scripture teaches that husbands and wives are to submit to each other out of reverence for Christ, and then it teaches us how to do that. Wives are to be honoring of their husbands as the head of the home and the representative of Christ. And husbands are to sacrificially and sensitively serve their wives just as Christ serves his bride, the Church.

Marriage is designed to work as an honoring partnership, without competition or dominance. In marriage, men and women are completely equal, but still different by God's design, and we each have specific biblical roles to fulfill.

Discuss what you think this looks like in the context of a healthy, functioning relationship. What does it look like for the husband to be the head of the home? And what does it look like for the wife to honor her husband as the representative of Christ while still living in equal partnership?

How should decisions regarding your home be made?

There are a lot of daily decisions that need to be made when navigating life together, and it's important to decide who will make those decisions in different areas. Who will decide which plumber to call when the sink stops up? Who will hire the exterminator? Who decides what is for dinner, and what time you're going to eat? What is the best way to fairly divide chores? Who is in charge of decorating? Even the smallest decisions can cause conflict if you haven't clearly defined how those things will be decided.

When you reach an impasse on a subject, how will you get past it?

No matter how well you have determined roles and divided up tasks, there will moments of impasse between you. When that time comes, who has the final say on a decision? When should the other spouse have veto power? And when (and who) should you call for outside help when you experience a problem in your marriage too great to reconcile on your own?

Discuss specific chores, and how you think they should be divided.

On a separate sheet of paper, write out your expectations when it comes to housework and chores. At the top of the paper, write, "I think I should do the following tasks…" Then on another sheet, write, "I think my spouse should do the following tasks…"

Have your potential mate do the same, then afterward, compare lists and see how well your expectations match. This is where negotiations may be in order.

CHAPTER FIFTEEN

LET'S TALK ABOUT KIDS

I (Jimmy) will often ask couples in pre-marriage counseling, "When you have children, who will be in charge of disciplining them?"

Invariably one of them will say, "Well, both of us, of course." The other will nod in agreement.

People instinctively understand that households run smoother when both parents take an equal role in disciplining children. But no matter how well-intentioned they are before having kids, it seldom works out that way. Usually one of them will become the disciplinarian, while the other is more interested in being the class clown.

Most often it is women who find themselves in the role of "bad cop," because their husbands usually default to the role of "good cop." Though sometimes those roles are reversed. It creates a lot of frustration in marriage, especially for the one who always ends up playing the "bad cop."

This was too often the case in my (Frank's) marriage, and it put a lot of undue stress on Ruthie. I'm embarrassed to say that I often defaulted to being the "good cop" when dealing with the kids, forcing Ruthie to become the heavy-handed disciplinarian. As the father, I should have been the one to take a firmer approach—especially when our kids were young and impressionable.

What children need most from their parents is a united front—not just in matters of discipline, but in every area of childrearing. When one parent abdicates his or her responsibilities, the other feels forced to step up and stand in the gap. The healthiest homes are those where both parents play equal roles in raising children—spiritually, physically, and emotionally.

> "BEFORE GETTING MARRIED, IT'S IMPORTANT TO COMMUNICATE YOUR EXPECTATIONS REGARDING CHILDREN, AND TO LEARN ALL YOU CAN ABOUT YOUR FUTURE PARTNER'S HOPES AND EXPECTATIONS."

Before getting married, it's important to communicate your expectations regarding children, and to learn all you can about your future partner's hopes and expectations. To help you get started, here are just a few of the many questions you should be discussing:

How many children would you like to have?

I (Jimmy) am amazed by how often couples have completely different ideas about the number of children they hope to have. Maybe he was a single child and enjoyed the attention, so he thinks one child is enough, while she has always dreamed of having five kids. Perhaps one of them doesn't want children, but the other doesn't know because they've never discussed it. If a compromise needs to be made, the time to make it is before you get married, not after.

How long do you hope to wait before having kids?

The vast majority of couples I counsel say they would like to wait several years before having children, but that's not always the case. Some people may want kids right away. Whatever the case, it's important to discuss the issue before marriage, just so you know you are both on the same page regarding your future family.

How do you feel about birth control? And how do you intend to "plan" your family?

Some people have religious objections to any type of birth control, while others see nothing wrong with it. Some may object to certain methods but be open to others. This is a matter of personal and Christian conviction, and should be discussed before marriage. Family planning is a joint decision, and whatever you decide needs to be a shared conviction between you and your spouse; otherwise it can cause a great deal of strife down the road.

What would happen if we couldn't have children for some reason?

Sometimes couples can't have children for medical reasons, and they don't find out that there is a problem until after they are married. Some couples in this situation choose to remain childless, while others turn to adoption.

It's important to talk about how important it is to have children of your own, and what you would do if that weren't possible. Is adoption a viable option for you? Would you look into foster parenting? Or would you be too devastated to consider any other options?

How should your children be educated?

There are many different options when it comes to educating children. Some have no problem with public school, while others prefer private schools, Christian schools, or home schooling. It may feel premature to talk about this issue now, but it's actually an important discussion to have. Private schools can be costly, and home schooling takes a tremendous amount of time and effort on the part of both parents. The type of schooling you decide can have an enormous impact on both your budget and lifestyle in the years to come. So take time to talk about it now.

How were you schooled as a child? Was it a good experience, or bad? And why? Do you hope to school your children in the same way, or did you have a different approach in mind?

What roles should both parents take when it comes to discipline?

Some people believe that the father should be the primary disciplinarian, while others believe that role should fall to the mother. Still others believe parents should take an equal role in the matter.

Talk about how you were disciplined as a child, and how that affected you. Who was the primary disciplinarian in your home? Was one parent the "good cop" while the other played the role of "bad cop?" Was this healthy? Confusing? Effective? And how have your experiences affected your thinking in this area?

What type of discipline is acceptable—and unacceptable?

How do you feel about spanking? Were you spanked as a child? How did you react to it? When is spanking acceptable, and when is it not? If you don't plan to spank your children, what type of discipline do you intend to use?

Spanking is a touchy issue these days, and a lot of people object to it. I personally believe it is a healthy and effective way to discipline, but only under very clearly-defined guidelines. It needs to be used only in the case of willful defiance, and on children who are old enough to understand exactly why they are being disciplined. And it should never be carried out in anger. Spanking should always be seen as a punishment for wrong behavior, and never as a way to vent or dominate.

You may have other thoughts and opinions on the subject, and so might your potential mate. It's a discussion you should have now, before having children together.

Is there a certain method or approach to childrearing that you intend to use?

Do you think children fare better in an atmosphere of permissiveness? Or do you plan to be more firm and disciplinarian? Is there a specific book or philosophy that you feel expresses the most effective model? Discuss your basic outlook on childrearing with your partner, and why you think certain methods are better than others.

How we handle children is often influenced heavily by our basic personalities. Someone who is outgoing and carefree, and always the life of the party, will almost always end up being the "fun" parent, while someone who is serious and pragmatic will tend to be more firm. But kids need stability and consistency from their parents, so it's important to establish your basic philosophies regarding childrearing, so as not to cause conflict and confusion.

How do you plan to train your children spiritually?

Do you intend to raise your children in a specific church or denomination? And what type of spiritual values and beliefs do you hope to instill in them? Does you potential mate share your convictions in this area?

Often dating couples have vastly differing religious views and opinions, and this doesn't cause a lot of conflict while they're simply dating. But these differences can create a lot of stress and confusion once children come along. Parents need to be on the same page spiritually in order to pass on those values to their children. It's easy for a Catholic to fall in love with a Presbyterian, but deciding which of those faiths to teach your children can be a source of conflict and turmoil.

Should children be allowed to make important decisions in the home, like where you go on vacation, where they will attend school, etc.?

When kids are young, they have very little say or influence over the family. Decisions made by the parents should be binding. But as they grow older, it's good to give them more say and responsibility in order to train them how to make good choices. Parenting is not about control; it's about nurturing kids toward independence. And this is done by slowly releasing the reins and allowing them more independence as they grow in maturity.

When kids reach middle school age, parents might consult them about their educational choices. Do they like the school they are attending, or would they like to look into other options?

Parents might also have a family meeting to discuss plans for an upcoming vacation. Perhaps they could give the children three choices for a fun vacation and then make the final decision through a family vote.

Discuss your views on growing independent children with your fiancé, and see how closely your thoughts align on the subject.

CHAPTER SIXTEEN

LET'S TALK ABOUT CAREERS

During pre-marriage counseling, I (Jimmy) once asked a couple, "Are you both going to work after the wedding?"

The young girl quickly answered, "No, I'm going to stay home with the children!"

Her fiancé gave her a surprised look. "I thought you were going to keep working! I don't make that much, and I thought we needed the money!"

"I'm going to stay home and raise the kids!" she said adamantly.

They got into an argument right there in my office. She eventually won. They went on to get married and today he works outside the home while she stays home to take care of the children. He had to trim back his expectations, but at least they worked through the issue before the wedding. Otherwise it could have been a tremendous source of conflict.

When it comes to career expectations, there are a lot of issues that couples need to talk through before getting married. Because what we do for a living and how we view our jobs has a marked impact on every aspect of the marriage.

For some people a career is just a job—a means of making a living. For others, their career is their identity. It's how they define their significance. Men are especially prone to finding their self-worth in what they do for a living. That's why the suicide rate is so high among executives who lose their jobs after spending their entire lives climbing the corporate ladder.

When your career is your identity, everything takes a back seat to the demands of work. And if you are engaged to such a person, it's something you need to know before signing on to playing second fiddle for the rest of your life.

Here are just a few of the issues you need to discuss at length before getting married.

How important is your career to you?

For some people, careers are intended to support the home, while others believe the home should support their careers. Some see jobs as nothing more than a means to an end. Others see jobs as the most important thing they do. These are things you need to know before getting married.

> "FOR SOME PEOPLE, CAREERS ARE INTENDED TO SUPPORT THE HOME, WHILE OTHERS BELIEVE THE HOME SHOULD SUPPORT THEIR CAREERS."

In a healthy home, careers should always take a back seat to more important matters, primarily your relationship with God, and the needs of your family—in that particular order. Make sure that you both have the same priorities—and right priorities—before making a mistake which you will most definitely regret.

Who was the primary breadwinner in your home growing up?

Our expectations regarding jobs and careers are often driven by our childhood experiences. Someone who saw their father go to work every day while their mother stayed home is more likely to expect that in their own family. Someone who grew up with a parent who was a workaholic may be resentful of a job that demands long hours. Or they may unthinkingly fall into that same pattern.

Discuss your childhood experiences in this area, and how those experiences have shaped your expectations.

Do you both plan to work outside the home, or will one of you stay home and take care of the children?

There is no right and wrong answer to this question, but it's important to understand both of your expectations and intentions going in. In some marriages the wife may be more career-oriented, so she becomes the primary breadwinner. In other homes that role falls to the husband. Still others decide that both spouses should work outside the home.

Whatever you decide, make sure it's a choice agreed upon by both partners.

In what way is your career tied to your life goals?

I (Frank) went into business for myself at a young age, and was in the process of building that business when Ruthie and I got married. My career was more than a job to me; it was the realization of a dream I'd had since childhood. I've always had a desire to be self-employed, and knew that it would take a lot of time and sacrifice to see that dream come to fruition.

Ruthie understood this desire, and was willing to come alongside me as we built the business together. Today we have a family business that I hope to pass onto my kids someday, and it has been a wonderful experience for us as a couple, but only because we've always worked to keep our priorities in perspective. Our business supports the family, but never trumps the needs of our family.

When your career is tied to a life-long goal or dream, it's difficult to keep it in proper perspective. It can easily become a monster that destroys your marriage. That's why it's important to talk about such things before standing at the altar.

Do you plan to stay in your present job? Or is it just a stepping-stone to something better?

Discuss your dreams for the future and your personal goals and desires when it comes to your career. Ask each other, "If you could have any job you wanted, what would it be?"

Often it is these kinds of discussions that lead us into careers we never dreamed we would have.

I (Frank) would likely have never written my first book if Ruthie hadn't asked me this exact question one night, just a few years into our marriage.

"I've always wanted to be a writer," I told her, and she never stopped encouraging me to try.

CHAPTER SEVENTEEN

LET'S TALK ABOUT MONEY

When I (Jimmy) first got married, I had a pretty immature view of money. I'd go to work each morning and spend my days selling appliances, then come home each evening and plop down in my favorite chair to watch television. I'd think to myself, I've done my job; now it's time for Karen to do hers.

I also assumed that since I was the sole breadwinner, I should have more say in how the money was spent. After all, it was my name on the paycheck.

Karen wasn't very happy with me back then, and I didn't have the mental bandwidth to understand why. Needless to say, God still had a lot to teach me about being equal partners in the marriage.

Money can be a huge blessing, or it can be a tremendous curse. Having too little money can easily lead to greed and envy, even destitution. While having too much money can lead to arrogance and pride. Money is not the root of evil, but the love of money is.

Your attitude toward money will have a marked impact on your relationship, and will likely create conflict in ways you never expected. So it's important to discuss your views and priorities regarding finances at length now, while your money is still in separate accounts.

Here are a few questions you should consider:

How important is money to you?

If you grew up in a rather wealthy family and have found yourself engaged to a blue-collar worker, chances are you have a lot of adjustments to make. Almost everyone says that money isn't important to them, but they quickly change their tune when they're down to their last few dollars. Money never feels important until you don't have enough to go around.

Discuss your attitude toward money, and how you've viewed money in the past. Have you always had plenty of money in the bank? Are you accustomed to living below your means? How would it affect your attitude if you had to live on less than you've always expected?

> "IN HEALTHY RELATIONSHIPS, MONEY IS BUDGETED THROUGH A GREAT DEAL OF PRAYER, DISCUSSION, AND COMPROMISE. BOTH SPOUSES HAVE AN EQUAL VOICE IN THE DECISION, AND GOD'S WILL AND WORD ARE ALWAYS RESPECTED IN THE DECISION-MAKING PROCESS."

Is a rewarding career more important than money?

Some people are more interested in finding a fulfilling career than in having a large bank account. A police officer, for instance, will likely never be paid as much as a corporate lawyer, but he may find a career in law enforcement far more gratifying. A schoolteacher who loves teaching kids might never be happy in a job that pays twice as much. A florist may not make as much as a doctor, but the lack of stress may be more than worth the tradeoff.

Is career more important than money to you? Or is career nothing more than a means of getting money? How you view your career will have a decided impact on your bank account, so it's important that you and your fiancé are on the same page.

How much money is enough?

Ask Bill Gates this question and you'll likely get an entirely different answer than your mail carrier might give. How much money is enough is a matter of perspective, and usually driven by how much we're accustomed to having.

But when entering into a new marriage, expectations are important to gauge. So talk about how much money is enough. How much do you make now? How secure is your job? Do you expect your income to grow, or to stay pretty much the same? Are we willing to live in a smaller house and drive one car if that's what it takes to get by?

Do you feel you have a healthy view of money?

When it comes to money, many people struggle with damaging inner vows. I (Frank) grew up extremely poor, and as a result, developed some very unhealthy inner vows as a child. I determined that I would never allow myself to be poor, and that thought became an inner vow that silently guided my life for many years as a young adult. It had a powerful hold on my life, and even today still haunts my thoughts and actions, even though I have long since recognized the problem, and even repented of it.

Do you have a healthy view of money? Or are you struggling with some damaging inner vows in this area? If so, how do you plan to break those vows before they do harm to your new marriage?

Who should have more say over how money is spent?

There is often an underlying belief that the one who brings home the paycheck in a marriage should have more say over how the money is spent. This was my (Jimmy's) basic understanding when Karen and I got married, and it caused a great deal of resentment during our first years together.

Marriage is a partnership—in every area. Though you may have different skills and roles, the partnership is still an equal one. One partner may become the primary breadwinner, but that doesn't mean they get to dominate the marriage. The breadwinner couldn't do their job without the support of their spouse.

In healthy relationships, money is budgeted through a great deal of prayer, discussion, and compromise. Both spouses have an equal voice in the decision, and God's will and word are always respected in the decision-making process.

Make sure that both you and your fiancé have a similar—and healthy—view when it comes to handling money.

When you are married, who should handle the finances?

Early in our marriage, I (Jimmy) kept a tight hold on our checkbook, but only because I had a need to control. Today Karen manages our bills, and she does a much better job of it than I ever did. We sit down regularly and set a clear budget, deciding how much we should allot toward tithes and offerings, how much we should put away in savings, and how much we have left over to spend, and then Karen takes that budget and makes it all work. She's very gifted when it comes to finances, and I'd rather spend my time doing things I'm better at, so the arrangement works well for our family.

> "FINANCIAL SETBACKS ARE A PART OF LIFE, AND THEY WILL COME INTO ALMOST EVERY MARRIAGE AT ONE TIME OR ANOTHER."

Talk about how you will handle your money once you get married. Otherwise you may find yourself fighting over control of the checkbook once your resources are pooled into one account.

How much should one partner be able to spend without getting the other's permission?

Can she buy a purse or a dress without first consulting him? Can he buy tools without first giving her a call? Can one buy a car without first getting permission from the other?

Talk about your expectations once you are living on the same budget. And be specific. Some women might expect to be consulted before the purchase of a pack of gum, while others wouldn't be upset if he showed up with a new boat.

Money is a limited resource in marriage, and it takes a lot of cooperation—and conversation—to establish a healthy balance of trust and teamwork.

How will we respond in the case of a job loss or financial crisis?

Financial setbacks are a part of life, and they will come into almost every marriage at one time or another. Discuss how you will handle money problems when they come along. Should the stay-at-home spouse look for work? Should the primary breadwinner take a second job so that it doesn't disrupt the schedule at home? Should you immediately cut back on expenses or sell your second car? Are you willing to move into a smaller home? Will you have put away savings so that none of these are necessary?

Real problems demand real solutions. So talk about it now and you'll be much better prepared in the future should you be faced with a financial crisis.

CHAPTER EIGHTEEN

LET'S TALK ABOUT IN-LAWS

I (Jimmy) remember once asking a young couple during pre-marriage counseling, "Where do you plan to spend your Christmas holidays?"

The young girl said, rather matter-of-factly, "With my family. We hate his family."

"We don't hate my family," the young man exclaimed.

"Yes we do!" she said. "We hate your family."

"Well, I don't hate them," he said.

"Yes you do," she told him. "You're always telling me how annoying they are."

They went back and forth like that for the next five minutes. I thought to myself, "That was the easiest can of worms I've ever opened."

This young couple had spent so much time talking about his dysfunctional family that she just assumed they'd be spending all their time with her family once they got married. But that was clearly news to him.

When it comes to dealing with in-laws, there are a lot of issues that need to be discussed. And those discussions need to be honest and open. When you marry someone, you are marrying into a family with a host of interpersonal dynamics already established. There could be a number of unresolved issues and resentments brewing beneath the surface that you would never see as an outsider. But once you are married, you're suddenly ushered into the inner circle. And the inner circle is where everything comes to light.

A family's inner circle can be a safe haven, or it can be a living nightmare. It also can be a little of both.

I've seen marriages literally torn apart by in-laws who don't know how to let go and couples who haven't learned to set healthy boundaries. And I've seen marriages saved through the careful intervention of godly and insightful parents. Your in-laws can be the best thing that ever happened to your marriage, or the bane of your existence. It's your job to understand the dynamics at work in both of your extended families, and to make decisions that are right for your immediate one.

Here are just a few of the many conversations you should be having with your potential mate.

How close are you to your parents?

Is your fiancé a "mama's boy" or a "daddy's girl?" Do they have a close but healthy relationship with their parents? Or are they too emotionally attached?

It's a good sign when your fiancé feels close to their parents. That usually means that they've had a happy and healthy childhood, with a minimal level of dysfunction. You want to think you are marrying into a family with strong family ties. But there's a point at which children can be too emotionally tied to their parents, and that can create a great deal of stress in your marriage.

Healthy boundaries are hard to set when your spouse is unwilling to cut any unhealthy apron strings. So make sure you have a clear understanding going in about any harmful emotional and psychological ties you may have to deal with.

How do your parents feel about the marriage?

When parents don't approve of your relationship, there's often a reason behind it.

Sometimes they may see red flags that you are choosing to ignore. Other times they may feel jealous of your partner, and are trying to hold onto the relationship you've always had with them. Still other times it is a sign that your parents are struggling to let go, and are acting out in fear of losing their child.

Regardless of the cause, if your parents don't approve of your relationship, there's a reason behind it that you need to look into. If they don't approve now, things will only get worse once you are married.

If you haven't had a frank and open discussion with your parents about their feelings, now is the time to do that. They may have some legitimate concerns, in which case you may need to reevaluate your plans for marriage. Or they may simply be hurt by something you've done or said. Then again, they may be acting out of unhealthy need or dysfunction.

Whatever the case, you won't know how to fix the problem until you get to the root of it. And this is one problem you need to work out before moving forward.

What do healthy boundaries with your in-laws—and parents—look like? And how do you plan to enforce them?

When it comes to dealing with in-laws, I (Jimmy) have a guiding principle that I try to pass on to every couple I counsel. I tell the husband, "It is your job to protect your wife from your parents. If they get out of line, or encroach on your family's space, or expect too much, it is your responsibility to confront them about it."

Then I tell the wife the same thing about her family. If her parents start to meddle in his private affairs, or put him down behind his back, it is her job to stand up to them, and then set healthy boundaries to keep it from happening again.

It's also important that couples never complain about each other to their parents. All that does is break the walls of confidentiality and invite them to participate in your drama. It's a breach of trust, and an open invitation to ignore any boundaries you've set in place.

Discuss the boundaries you plan to implement, as well as your strategy for enforcing them.

How will you divide your time between the two families?

One of the greatest sources of conflict and hurt feelings in new marriages comes when couples decide to spend Christmas or Thanksgiving with their "other" parents. When you've spent every holiday at home with your family and then suddenly decide to spend New Year's Eve with your spouse's parents, it's almost impossible to do so without your parents feeling a little slighted.

But this is what "leaving and cleaving" is all about. And both sets of parents have to get used to the idea of sharing you with others. It's a tight walk that every newly married couple has to navigate.

It softens the blow if you talk about it before the wedding, and then discuss your future plans with both sets of parents, so they aren't caught off guard. One good compromise is to alternate your holiday plans from year to year, like spending Christmas with his family and Thanksgiving with hers, then reversing that the following year.

Obviously this is easier to navigate if both sets of parents live in the same town, but even then you have to be fair with your time, and creative in the way you schedule your holiday activities.

If you all live in the same area, you'll have even more work to do. Who will you visit on the weekends, or have lunch with on Sundays? How many visits a week are acceptable? If you have dinner with his family, do you owe hers dinner soon after? It can wear you out if you let it, so make sure you don't.

This is part of setting healthy boundaries. The key is to be as fair as you can, communicate your plans well, and don't allow guilt trips to guide your decisions.

What role will your parents and in-laws play in the lives of your children?

When my (Jimmy's) kids were young, my parents were very loving grandparents, but they were not believers, and we had some rules for our children that my parents didn't understand. For example, our kids were not allowed to watch many of the shows on television, so whenever we would allow my parents to babysit, I'd tell my mom and dad which shows we didn't want our children to watch. The minute we left, they would let them watch anything they wanted. We found out because our kids would always tell on them later.

We had to set some tight boundaries with my parents when it came to spending time our children, and they weren't always happy about it. But it was an important decision to make, because I couldn't allow them to undermine my authority as a parent.

You may need to make some tough decisions of your own. Then again, you may be looking forward to your kids spending time with parents. That's something only you and your future spouse can decide.

How much time do you want your kids to spend around your parents? What about your fiancé's parents? Do you trust them to be good influences? Or do you already know this is going to be a problem area when you have children? Discuss these things now so that you can start early putting a plan of action in place.

What will you do when your parents or in-laws can't take care of themselves?

No one likes to think about their parents getting older, but it's a reality that we all face. And when that happens, someone may have to step in and care for them. Make sure you and your spouse are on the same page when it comes to caring for elderly parents.

How do you feel about your parents moving in with you? What about your spouse's parents? Is a retirement center a viable option? What if they can't afford to take care of themselves? Are you willing take on the added financial expense?

These are issues most of us have to deal with sooner or later. It's better to talk about them now, so there won't be any surprises in the future.

CHAPTER NINETEEN

LET'S TALK ABOUT SEX

Here's the dichotomy about sex and marriage:

When you're single, you can't wait to get married, so you can have all the sex you want. But you know in your heart that it's not the "be all and end all" that Hollywood films have made it out to be. If you're engaged, chances are good that most of your married friends have already told you that—especially if you're a virgin.

"You think that sex is going to be this big deal," they say, "and then you get married and find out it's really not that important. Of course, it's fun, but you can't spend all your time in bed. It's just one small part of your marriage."

The truth is, your friends are partly right. Sex is only a small part of your relationship. What they're not telling you, though, is it's one of the most important parts of your relationship—even if it is just a few hours a week.

Sex is the superglue of marriage. Once you figure out how to do it (and trust me, you will have to figure out what you're doing), you find that sex is the most intimate and satisfying experience that you could ever imagine having with another human being.

First of all, it's so much fun! Most couples can't get enough during the first few months of marriage. Who knew a king sized bed and a handful of pillows could lead to so many possibilities?

And second, it is a heart-binding experience. It brings a level of intimacy and connection and trust that no activity on earth could possibly provide. When you are able to give yourself freely to another person, with no guilt, no reservation, no hint of shame or remorse, it creates a bond that is complete and incomparable. It fully engages you in the relationship. And yes, it is a highly spiritual experience. Because that is how God intended it.

Talking about sex with your future spouse may feel awkward, and may be a little pre-mature or inappropriate—especially if you're already struggling to keep your hands where they belong. My advice to younger couples would be to hold off discussing these things in private, and instead bring them up in the company of your pastor or counselor during pre-marriage counseling.

But if you feel comfortable, are a bit older, and don't feel it will lead to unnecessary temptation, here are a few important questions to get you started.

How important is sex to you?

When it comes to sex, men and women have entirely different needs and expectations. A woman's view of romance is tied directly to her emotional needs and her desire to connect with her husband. She needs to be cuddled and caressed and complimented. She longs for non-sexual touch and affection. She gets turned on by seeing her husband help around the house, or finding an unexpected love letter under her pillow.

> "DURING SEX, WE CONNECT WITH EACH OTHER SPIRITUALLY, EMOTIONALLY, AND PHYSICALLY. WE BECOME ONE IN HEART, MIND, AND BODY."

A man's view of romance, however, is much less complicated. Is she naked? And did she bring nachos? That's all he needs to know.

Sex is important to both men and women, but for entirely different reasons.

And usually to varying degrees.

Talk about your differing expectations when it comes to sex. Ask, "On a scale of 1 to 10, how important do you think sex will be in our marriage?" And compare your answers. Talk about what does and doesn't turn you on, as well as what turns you off. If he has chronic bad breath now, that is likely to become a huge problem with you in bed, so maybe now is the time to lovingly bring it up.

You might also discuss things that might present a problem with your future spouse. For instance, if a man hasn't been circumcised, it would be good to bring that up before marriage. It may not be an issue, but for some women, that could be a problem.

How often do you think we'll be having sex?

One of the biggest misconception couples have before marriage is that if the relationship is strong, they should have the same desire for sex. They expect to be perfectly in sync, always wanting sex at the same time, and in the same manner. But it rarely happens that way.

In marriage, it's often one partner that needs sex, while the other accommodates them. This is especially true as you get older.

Of course sex is always fun, even when you aren't particularly in the mood. And once you get started, it's not hard to get into the swing of things. But if you only had sex when both of you were equally turned on, you'd almost never have sex—at least in most relationships.

In marriage, sex is where your servant spirit should kick into high gear. The best sexual relationships are between two people committed to meeting each other's needs and desires, regardless of how they happen to feel at a given moment. Great sex happens when a man learns all he can about his wife's need for touch and affection and romance, and sets out to meet those needs. And it happens when a wife becomes dialed into her husband's unique needs and desires, and willingly accommodates those needs.

He does the dishes and brings her flowers for no apparent reason, and she shows up naked with nachos. That's what it looks like when two servants fall in love.

How often you have sex is dependent entirely on your differing needs and expectations, and it takes a great deal of communication to learn those things. Those discussions should start now and continue well into your marriage. As your marriage progresses, your sexual needs will change, so it takes continual communication to keep your sex life healthy and on track.

Are you willing to meet a need in your spouse that you don't have? And is your potential mate willing to do the same? That's what you most need to consider if you expect to have a healthy and vibrant sex life.

What purpose do you think sex serves in marriage?

Did you know that humans are the only species that face each other during sex? What does that tell you about God's intent when he designed us?

It tells us that sex between a husband and wife is as much about relation as it is procreation.

With animals, sex is about keeping the circle of life moving forward. They have sex to keep their species from dying out, but that's the only real point to it. That's not the case with you and me. Humans were designed to be highly relational. Our desire for sex serves a much higher purpose, and fills a much greater void.

During sex, we connect with each other spiritually, emotionally, and physically. We become one in heart, mind, and body. God literally binds our hearts together in a very spiritual, almost supernatural way. In God's economy, sex between a husband and wife is a divine and transcendent act. That's one of the reasons why sex outside of marriage is such an affront to God's purpose and design. Because you and I are not animals, and sex is far more than a physical event.

Sex in marriage also keeps temptation at bay. A man's need for sex is a powerful force, and most men face temptation at every turn and corner. Pornography is always just a click away, and the voices promising sexual fulfillment are never ending. It's no wonder that every warning of sexual temptation in the book of Proverbs is directed at men. Women are not immune to temptation, but men are Satan's primary targets, and it is a wife's job to understand that reality so that she can help counter it.

Sex does more than bind your hearts together; it keeps your hearts from wavering. That's why it's so important to discuss your individual needs and desires, and to talk about what purpose sex will serve in your marriage.

What is your greatest need when it comes to sex? What can I do to keep that need fulfilled? Do you promise to tell me if you ever feel sexually frustrated or unfulfilled?

Have you ever had sex? Or are you still a virgin?

We serve a forgiving God who doesn't hold our past against us, and we should always be willing to forgive others of their past sins. But all sins bring some form of consequence, and one of the many consequences of sexual sins is having to confess them to our future spouse. Your sexual past can have a marked impact on your future relationship, and your partner deserves your complete honesty and openness in this area.

Have you been sexually active in the past? Was it a one-time act, or an ongoing relationship? How many partners have you had? Are there any sexual diseases or infections you will have to worry about? Have you been tested for sexually transmitted diseases? In what ways are you afraid your past might inhibit or affect your sexual behavior in the future? Have you ever had a problem with pornography? Do you have a problem with it now?

> "THE BEST SEXUAL RELATIONSHIPS ARE BETWEEN TWO PEOPLE COMMITTED TO MEETING EACH OTHER'S NEEDS AND DESIRES, REGARDLESS OF HOW THEY HAPPEN TO FEEL AT A GIVEN MOMENT."

Have you ever been sexually abused or mistreated?

I (Jimmy) once counseled an attractive young couple that struggled to stay pure during their engagement. They were honest with me about their temptations, so every time they sat across from me I threatened to hang him by his toenails if he didn't keep his hands off of her until the wedding. They did remain pure, and I was proud of them for it.

Then several months into their wedding they came to me with tears in their eyes, asking for help. They still had not had sexual relations because she simply wasn't able to open up to him.

I soon discovered that her grandfather had sexually abused her as a child. For years he would sneak into her bed at night and force himself on her, and she had blocked the experience—until the first night of their honeymoon. Her husband reached over to touch her and she completely shut down. Her abuse had caused her to become physically and emotionally frigid.

They were able to work through the problem, but it took a lot of counseling, patience, and sensitivity.

These are things that need to come to light before the wedding, because they can do great harm afterward. Have you ever been the victim of abuse—sexually, verbally, or emotionally? Have you ever been subjected to sexual abuse—through violent pornography, video games, or abuse in your household? Have you ever had violent or deviant tendencies? If so, where do you think those tendencies came from, and what is your plan of action to deal with it?

What type of sex is acceptable—and unacceptable—in marriage?

In Christian circles, there are as many thoughts about what is and isn't acceptable and healthy when it comes to sex as there are sexual positions. A legalistic view might say that sex should only be for the purpose of procreation, while a liberal view might be closer to a secular school of thought than a biblical one.

My (Jimmy's) advice on the subject is simple and direct. When couples come to me for advice on this topic, I tell them that if the Bible doesn't clearly speak against a sexual activity, then God is not going to be displeased by it. Sometimes the Bible speaks clearly on a subject by not speaking on it at all.

In marriage, sex is like a huge playground that God has designed and set aside for a couple's pleasure and enjoyment, and there are a lot of different ways to have fun. But that playground has a well-defined fence around it to keep you safe. The Bible outlines specifically what those perimeters should be. Those things that God considers harmful or immoral or unnatural are clearly addressed in scripture, and it's a good idea to study those things so that you won't be led astray.

But if the Bible doesn't speak against a certain sexual act or desire, and if it is safe, and something you both enjoy, I tell people to lock the door, dig out your Batman costume, and have at it!

The important thing is to make sure it's something you both want, and that it doesn't feel offensive or degrading to either of you. But it's an important topic to discuss.

What are your sexual desires and fantasies? What can I do to better please you during sex? Is there anything you think will make you feel uncomfortable or shameful? What are your favorite sexual positions and activities? What stimulates you the most—and the least?

Once again, this may be a topic better reserved for the privacy of your bedroom after the wedding, but when the proper time comes, don't allow yourself to be too bashful to bring these things up.

CHAPTER TWENTY

LET'S TALK ABOUT OUR SPIRITUAL LIVES

My (Jimmy's) good friend Tom Lane has a litmus test he uses when couples come to him for counseling. At the beginning of their first session, he asks them two specific questions. "What is your commitment to Christ? And what is your commitment to your marriage?"

If they can't answer both of those questions to his satisfaction, he refuses to counsel them. Tom is not a negative or judgmental person, and he's certainly not unkind, he just knows that he can't really help a couple that isn't fully committed to Christ and wholly committed to their marriage.

If a couple is not completely sold out to Jesus, nothing about their marriage really matters. They may stay together, but that doesn't mean that they have a truly fruitful or meaningful relationship. And there is no real point to their marriage. No matter what they do, or how long they stay married, it will always be about their own selfish needs and desires.

If God is not at the center of your life, your life will never be fully centered.

And the same is true for your marriage.

When it comes to your spiritual life and your personal relationship with God, you need a marriage partner who will walk that journey alongside you. Not one who will potentially hold you back or steer you away. There is no way to overthink this issue. Before going to the altar, make sure you've had some open and honest discussions regarding your spiritual beliefs, desires, and commitments. And be honest with yourself about your partner's spiritual dedication. If he isn't leading you spiritually while you are single, what makes you think he will do so when you are married?

Tell me about your spiritual journey and testimony.

If you haven't learned all you can about your potential mate's spiritual depth and relationship with God, it's time to have that discussion. Too many people today are living life as nominal believers. They wear the label "Christian," but not much about their life reflects that claim. If you are serious about your faith, and your partner isn't, you will spend the rest of your life regretting the day you exchanged rings with a person who doesn't share your level of commitment.

Being married to a lukewarm Christian is not much different than being married to an unbeliever. It may even be worse. So make sure now that you are equally yoked.

When did you first come to Jesus? How has that commitment impacted your life? In what ways has God changed your life? Do you ever have doubts? Do you spend time reading God's word? What do you do to keep your relationship with God intact and growing?

How important is church attendance to you? And where will we attend church?

My wife often tells a story from her days in college. Her favorite Bible teacher was an older professor who often did more mentoring in the classroom than teaching.

One day he stepped down from his teaching platform in order to get a better view, and then scanned the room to make sure he had everyone's attention. She said that whenever he did that, the class knew that they were about to hear something really important.

After a long, solemn pause, he said, "Men, don't you ever get out of the habit of taking your family to church. You are the spiritual leader of your home, and you need to lead by example. If you don't like your church, find one you do like, and every time the doors are open, you have your family there!"

He paused again to let his words sink in. Then he continued. "And women, make sure you marry a man who will wake up your family every Sunday morning so that everyone can get dressed, and then stand at your bedroom door and say, 'Wife, get your hat on, cause it's time to go to church!'"

Her old professor wasn't a legalist, but he understood a powerful spiritual principle. We

"IF YOU HAVEN'T LEARNED ALL YOU CAN ABOUT YOUR POTENTIAL MATE'S SPIRITUAL DEPTH AND RELATIONSHIP WITH GOD, IT'S TIME TO HAVE THAT DISCUSSION."

need fellowship with other believers in order to survive. And it's the husband's responsibility to see that the family gets the spiritual fellowship they need.

How important is church to you? How important is it that your kids go to church regularly? How involved do you plan to be in your church fellowship? Are you going to be committed to church attendance as a family? And which church do you plan to attend regularly?

What is our prayer life going to look like?

Couples who pray together on a daily basis are far more likely to be happy and fulfilled and committed to the marriage than those who don't. That is a fact that's been proven time and again in research. But I don't need a study to tell me how true that is. I (Jimmy) see it every day in the lives of my friends, co-workers, and in the congregation I pastor.

Any time you see a strong and vibrant marriage, at the heart of it is two deeply committed Christians who spend quality time together every day in prayer and spiritual communion.

Prayer is the lifeblood of your relationship with God. And when you pray together, it becomes the lifeblood of your marriage.

How often do you spend time in prayer and Bible study? Are you committed to praying with me on a daily basis? Will our family pray together daily? How do you plan to teach our children to pray? What will we pray about as a couple? What will we pray for as a family? Will prayer play a part in all of our family decisions? Will we have regular devotions as a family? Who should be the one in charge of making those devotions happen?

Do we share the same spiritual beliefs and convictions?

Can a charismatic Christian marry a cessationist and still be happy? It's a question that comes up more often than you might think. And I hear other variations of it as well. Can a Catholic marry a Protestant? Can a Southern Baptist marry a Mormon? Should a Presbyterian marry a Jehovah's Witness?

Each time I hear these questions I think of Tevye's response to his daughter Chava in Fiddler on the Roof. They were a devout Jewish family, and she had fallen in love with a Russian Gentile named Fyedka. "A bird may love a fish, but where would they make a home?" Tevye asked her.

His point was simple. Often we think that love will overcome all our differences, but at the end of the day, these things really do matter. Especially in the context of marriage.

This may sound harsh, but if you have found yourself engaged to someone who doesn't share your core spiritual convictions and beliefs, it's likely because your faith is not really that important to you. The fact that you have made a decision to marry someone with deeply conflicting spiritual practices and opinions means that your convictions are negotiable. They are not really your core beliefs, just something you profess to believe.

A passionate, practicing charismatic Christian will never be happy living with a nominal Catholic. They are unequally yoked, and should never consider getting married.

Having said that, it's important to define which spiritual differences will and won't matter. Obviously, there are many beliefs in the Christian faith that are based more on theological opinion than foundational convictions. What you believe about the end times, or how you interpret the Book of Revelation is highly subjective, and not really a matter of principle. They are simply differences in interpretation. But every faith has essential convictions that should never be compromised.

In the Christian faith, these core convictions are clearly revealed in scripture, and considered essential beliefs for anyone who claims to follow Christ as their Savior. We believe in the virgin birth of Jesus, in the deity of Christ, and salvation by grace alone through the blood of Jesus shed on the cross. We believe in the physical death, burial, and resurrection of Jesus, for the atonement of sins. We believe in the inerrancy of Scripture, and in one God, manifested through the Holy Trinity: Father, Son, and Holy Spirit.

For a Bible-believing follower of Christ, these are not open to debate. They are core essentials to the Christian faith, and should not be taken lightly. If you don't share these convictions with your potential mate, you may have some serious soul searching to do.

CHAPTER
TWENTY-ONE

LET'S TALK ABOUT REMARRIAGE
AND PREVIOUS RELATIONSHIPS

I (Jimmy) had a close friend in high school that married his high school sweetheart. They were great together, and got married right out of college. But he had always had a drinking problem, and it got worse as they grew older.

His wife stuck with him for as long as she could, but eventually his alcoholism destroyed their marriage. He died just a few years after their divorce.

She remarried a wonderful man, and I saw her a few years later at a soccer game. I congratulated her on her new marriage and asked how she was doing.

"We're doing great," she said. "We're very happy." Then she paused for a second, took a step closer and added, "But I still love my first husband."

She was able to go on with her life, but even after years of pain and heartache, she still had a place in her heart for her first love.

Research shows that more than 50% of divorcees who have been divorced for ten years or more say they still love their first spouse—even when the divorce was a cruel and bitter one. You never quite get over the first person you willingly let into your heart.

Someone once said that when a heart breaks, it seldom breaks evenly. There is a part of your heart that always stays with the people you've let inside. When you have sexual intimacy with another person, you've become one with them. You have literally bound your heart, soul, and body to theirs. Once that happens, separation is never fully possible. It's like melting two candles together and then trying again to make two candles out of them. It can't really be done. They will always carry pieces of each other inside.

That's why God hates divorce. And it's why remarriage after divorce should never be taken lightly.

Divorce and remarriage is a highly-charged subject in the Christian community, and there are many differing views on what the Bible does and doesn't teach on the subject. We're not going to have that debate here, because it's something you need to be working through with your church pastor or counselor. What we plan to do here is give you some specific things to think through and talk about if you're considering a remarriage.

My only strong word of advice is this: Don't allow yourself to remarry unless you are fully comfortable with your decision, and until you feel God's release and blessing to do so.

"OFTEN ON THE HEELS OF DIVORCE, OUR PAIN CAUSES US TO MAKE DANGEROUS AND DESTRUCTIVE PROMISES TO OURSELVES."

If you made mistakes in your first marriage, you need time to deal with them and make sure they are truly in your past. You also need to have made things right with your ex-partner—at least as far as possible. If you were abused, abandoned, cheated on, or sinned against in any other way, you need time to heal and forgive in order to be healthy enough for another relationship. If you are marrying someone who was married before, you need to make sure that they have overcome the baggage from their past relationship, and are healthy enough for another marriage.

God is a forgiving God, and he doesn't want us to live in guilt or shame. And because of his great love for us, he wants our future to be brighter than our past. For that to happen, our pain needs to be fully laid to rest before we move forward.

Here are just a few of the questions you need to be asking and talking about with your potential new partner.

What caused the breakup of your first marriage?

If you haven't thoroughly discussed the dynamics and problems of your first marriage with your new partner, it's important to do so before moving forward. They need to know everything they can about your past marriage, even though it may feel uncomfortable to talk about. If there are mistakes you made, be honest with them about those mistakes, and talk about what you have done to keep those negative patterns from repeating. Chances are pretty good that you've spent a lot of time talking about what an idiot your ex-spouse was, but it's also important to be honest about your own failings.

In what ways did you add to the conflict in your first marriage? How do you plan to do things differently in your second marriage? What makes you think those patterns of behavior won't be repeated?

How do your family members feel about your new marriage?

Don't be surprised if people in your family have a problem with your new marriage. If you have kids, they may still be hurting from the divorce, and really struggling to accept your new partner. If they are grown children, they likely have concerns that they're not discussing with you, like how this new marriage will affect their inheritance, holidays, and the time they get to spend with you. Will they have to share you with people they don't even know? Will you like your new family better than you like them? Will everyone get along?

Your parents may wonder why you are risking getting into another bad relationship. Your siblings may be smiling to your face but inwardly thinking you are making a mistake.

If you haven't talked openly and honestly with those closest to you to make sure they understand your decision, it's important to do so. You may feel you don't need their approval and blessing, but it sure makes life easier if you have it.

Why do you believe this marriage will work when your previous one didn't?

There are realities about second marriages that you simply can't gloss over.

First of all, the divorce rates are higher in cases of remarriage. This doesn't mean that you can't succeed, just that you need to be aware of the special challenges that need to be addressed.

Second, you will face obstacles that your first marriage didn't have to deal with. Second marriages begin with a lot more players, and that brings some special baggage into the relationship. There are often two ex-spouses on the scene, which means four sets of parents, and children from two previous marriages. There are financial ties that have to be considered.

Third, you may be starting your life together with kids still in the home, and sometimes those kids are not emotionally healed from a prior marriage. You may have a more difficult time finding time to be alone. And you'll also be navigating family dynamics that are already established.

The term "newlywed" may not feel like it applies to you, because you've done it all before. This can be a challenging environment in which to navigate a new marriage, and it's important that you understand that truth in order to prepare for it.

How are we going to make this work? What boundaries are we going to put into place to make sure the stress doesn't overtake our relationship? What do we need to do to protect each other from our previous spouses and in-laws? Can we commit to always having a united front when it comes to both your children and mine?

Have the wounds from your first marriage fully healed?

The devil is very evil, and he works overtime to destroy marriages. When we divorce, he begins whispering messages of disgrace, regret, and humiliation into our hearts over the breakup, making us feel like failures. Satan isn't happy until we're all reeling in regret and defeat.

Bad marriages also leave behind a lot of damaging inner vows. Often on the heels of divorce, our pain causes us to make dangerous and destructive promises to ourselves. I'll never let anyone hurt me like that again. No one is ever going to take me for granted! I'll never be talked to like that again!

These inner vows are damaging and dangerous, and they can easily destroy another marriage if you don't deal with them.

Have you found healing from your divorce in order to move forward? Are you sure the pain in your spirit has been dealt with? How certain are you that these things won't come back and haunt you in the future? Have you broken any negative inner vows you made in response to a previous marriage or relationship?

Have you dealt with the sins of your first marriage?

If you were the one who left your first partner, or caused your marriage to fail through adultery, or emotional unfaithfulness, or other personal sins, have you repented of your failings? Have you taken responsibility for your actions, and owned your role in the breakup? Have you taken steps to get help or spiritual healing? Have you been through counseling? Are you a different person? How do you know you won't repeat your past patterns of sin?

"GOD IS A FORGIVING GOD, AND HE DOESN'T WANT US TO LIVE IN GUILT OR SHAME."

God doesn't rub our noses in our mistakes, and we shouldn't either. But he does expect us to repent and change on the heels of moral failure. If you haven't fully owned your sins before God and your potential mate, and found healing for those sins, you shouldn't remarry until that happens.

This is no small matter, and you owe it to your future spouse to find healing and forgiveness before binding your heart to theirs.

Was your previous relationship a co-habitation, or a sexual relationship?

In some cases, there is no first marriage in the past, but a co-habitation, or a sexual relationship, or even an adulterous affair. There is no divorce to deal with, but there are still sexual, spiritual, and emotional ties that are bound to affect your upcoming marriage in a negative way. These types of ties can be just as damaging and destructive as a bad marriage, and the emotional baggage can be just as difficult to overcome. Whenever you have sexual relations with another person, even outside of marriage, there is a soul-tie that happens. And there are consequences to not taking the needed steps to fully breaking that tie.

If this is your situation, have you repented of your past sins? Have you completely broken off communication with the other person? Have you found spiritual and emotional healing? Is the affair over for good? What boundaries have you put into place to make sure your previous relationship is fully over? Have you broken any damaging inner vows you made on the heels of your affair? Have you taken spiritual authority over your life to keep the devil from tormenting you through condemnation, shame, and lies? In order to put your past in the past, you will need to take a stand spiritually and move forward with your faith in God.

CHAPTER TWENTY-TWO
LET'S TALK ABOUT BLENDED FAMILIES

In the United States alone, more than 1.2 million people a year get divorced, and about seventy-five percent of them eventually get remarried. The majority of them bring children into the second marriage, and they quickly discover that stepfamily life is far more complicated than they expected. There are new schedules to navigate, squabbling siblings to discipline, ex-spouses who still play a role in the children's lives, and a new spouse who has never been a parent to your children. The challenges can feel overwhelming, and often take a tremendous toll on the new marriage.

In a traditional first marriage, kids have grown up with their biological parents, so there are no divided loyalties to deal with. The kids understand that they have to obey both parents. But when a new parent steps into the picture, they not only can feel resentful, but jealous that now they have to compete for their parent's attention. That's why it is wise to make children feel like part of the relationship as early as possible. They need to feel informed and safe as the relationship forms.

If you are considering remarriage and there are children in the picture, there are a lot of discussions you need to be having beforehand, both with your spouse and all of the children involved.

Are you fully prepared for the ride ahead?

Most experts say it takes between two and five years for a stepfamily to fully establish itself. That doesn't mean you can't have fulfilling family dynamics for that period, but it does mean you have to be patient, and have realistic expectations. Otherwise you could get frustrated and feel like you are failing, even when you aren't. In blended family relationships, things often take a little longer, but in the end, can be just as fulfilling and successful.

No matter how well you navigate the dynamics of your new blended family, there will be some challenges and surprises. So be prepared to show a lot of patience and tenacity.

Have you been consistently praying about your new relationship? Have you talked to your new partner about your fears and concerns, or any red flags you might be seeing? Have you steadied yourself emotionally and are you determined to do whatever it takes to make the new marriage work?

Are you willing to let your new spouse have authority over your children? And are you willing to give them authority over yours?

I (Jimmy) once counseled a remarried couple just a few months into their new marriage, and the man told me he was at the end of his rope. Her children simply refused to accept him as their new father. They were a great couple, and seemed to be highly compatible, but her kids were making him miserable. They were attacking him verbally, and insulting him each time he tried to discipline them.

"I love my wife," he said in frustration, "but I can't deal with her children anymore. You can't imagine how bad it is. They are killing me!"

His wife confirmed his complaints, so I asked her, "Why are you letting your children get away with this?"

She let out a deep sigh. "They've just been through so much since I divorced their father, I don't want them to be hurt again," she said.

I couldn't believe my ears. "So you're telling me you married a man that you don't trust with your children?" I asked her. "You realize this is not just some man living in your house. This is your husband. He has to be the priority in your life, and he has to have authority over your children, or this will never work."

She thought for a few minutes, then shook her head and said, "I can't do that to my kids. I can't allow him to do that."

We spent over an hour discussing the problem, but she was unwilling to give in. They decided to separate that day in my office. It was sad to see, because I think they could have made the marriage work. But she simply wasn't willing to give her husband authority over her children.

This issue should have been resolved long before they decided to get married. So make sure that the same thing doesn't happen to you. Have you discussed this issue with your new spouse and agreed to give them authority over your children? Have you settled in your heart that they will be disciplining your children as well? Are you emotionally prepared to stand in unity with your new spouse in all areas of discipline and correction?

> "ARE YOU EMOTIONALLY PREPARED TO STAND IN UNITY WITH YOUR NEW SPOUSE IN ALL AREAS OF DISCIPLINE AND CORRECTION?"

Who should discipline your children—and theirs?

It is best in blended families for the biological parent to enforce discipline over their own children. This is especially important when the marriage is new. But children still need to understand that they are under the authority of both parents, and a stepparent still has the right to enforce discipline. You are equal partners when it comes to enforcing rules. A stepparent needs to assert authority over the children, but should be careful not to try to replace their biological parent, or in any way disrespect them.

Children have a natural loyalty to their biological parents, and it's important to respect that relationship. They may not want to call you "mom" or "dad" out of a sense of loyalty to their biological parent, and that's a very natural response. You should respect their desire in that area, while still training them to respect you as their stepparent.

Talk about how you will handle matters of discipline when they arise. Are you willing to take the lead role in disciplining your biological children? Are you willing to defer to your spouse when it comes to disciplining their children? How will you handle situations where the children disrespect either stepparent?

Have you discussed this with your kids, so that there is no confusion on the matter?

Sometimes couples go into a new marriage assuming that their children are on board, only to find out that the kids are deeply resentful. This is especially true when kids are older.

One man at our church decided to remarry a woman who had teenage children, and he thought that they were okay with the new marriage. But he learned otherwise on the day of their wedding. Just before the ceremony, her oldest son walked up to him and said, "I want you to know that I'm going to make your life a living hell from this day forward."

> "AS THEIR BIOLOGICAL PARENT, IT'S YOUR ROLE TO PROTECT YOUR NEW SPOUSE FROM THEM, AND TO LEAVE NO DOUBT WHICH SIDE YOU WILL BE TAKING ONCE THERE IS ANOTHER PARENT IN THE HOUSE."

And that's exactly what he did. The day after the wedding the children began acting out, and they never accepted him as their new father.

This should have been worked out long before they decided to get married. If you have children, it's your job to see that they fully understand the changes that will soon be taking place. As their biological parent, it's your role to protect your new spouse from them, and to leave no doubt which side you will be taking once there is another parent in the house.

Have you fully prepared your kids for your new marriage? Have you explained to them that once you are married, you expect them to obey their new parent without question? Have you discussed this with them in the company of your new partner? If not, it may be in order to call a family meeting, and to include your future spouse, so that you can all discuss it together.

Have you discussed your views on family rules and discipline with your future spouse?

Kids need consistency from their parents; otherwise they become confused and frustrated. One of the greatest reasons kids act out is that they sense areas of inconsistency or vulnerability, and they are testing the limits in those areas. This is especially true in stepfamilies, where new parents are suddenly on the scene. It's important to go into your new marriage with a very clear consensus regarding the family rules and boundaries, and what form of discipline will be used when kids don't comply.

What type of discipline have you used in the past with your children? Is your new spouse in agreement with your rules? Do they share your views and values on what types of discipline are acceptable—and unacceptable? Are you okay with spanking? Or do you prefer a time-out method?

Talk at length on this subject before going into marriage, so you know you're both on the same page from day one of the marriage.

Are you willing to make your marriage your top priority?

This is a guiding principle that I (Jimmy) teach as the top priority in the home. And that's true whether it is a first marriage or a re-marriage. Once the rings have been exchanged, all other priorities take a back seat to your commitment to each other—except, of course, your relationship with God.

Children instinctively fight this rule. Especially when it's a new parent in the home. Often they have been the top priority in your life—or your future spouse's life—and they won't appreciate being moved back one seat on the bus. But if you don't establish this rule from the beginning of the marriage, and let the children know exactly where your new spouse stands, you are in for a lot of conflict and struggle for control.

Have you settled in your heart that your new spouse will become your most important earthly relationship? Have you talked to your kids about this? Have you committed to your future spouse that no matter what needs or demands vie for your attention, that they will always come first?

If you get the first law of marriage right, every other priority in your marriage will naturally fall into place. So write it down in the front of your Bible and never forget it.

God first. Your spouse second. Children third. Everything else after that.

CHAPTER TWENTY-THREE

LET'S TALK ABOUT COMMITMENT

Statistics show that about half of all couples decide to live together before marriage. If that's true, then it's fair to assume that a good number of single people reading this book are presently cohabitating.

Some might be engaged to be married and living together in order to save expenses while they plan their wedding. Others might be long-time companions who have considered getting married some day, but have just never taken that next step. Still others might be children of divorce who are afraid to get married, because they know how painful a divorce can be. They know in their hearts that it's wrong, but they can't bear the thought of getting into a bad marriage, so they decided instead to simply live together.

Whatever the cause, we're aware that cohabitation is far more common and accepted today than it used to be, and that means you may very well be in that situation. If so, then I hope you won't skip over this chapter, because we have some advice we really want you to hear.

As a pastor, I (Jimmy) increasingly see cohabitating couples in our church services, and many of them have grown up in the church. It's obvious that many believers know what the Bible has to say about sex before marriage, but they willfully choose to disobey. Either they think the practice of marriage is outdated, or they know that they are in the wrong but just don't care.

Others may not have grown up in the church, so they don't really understand the biblical view on the subject. Many of their friends live together, so they see nothing wrong with the lifestyle. In those cases it's my job as a pastor to teach them.

Regardless of their situation, I'm at least glad to see them at church, because that shows they have something of an interest in following God's will and desire for them as a couple. They simply haven't quite grasped how strongly God feels about marriage, and how much he longs to see them in a covenantal relationship.

If any of this describes you, I'm glad that you've found yourself on this page, because that tells me that you, too, have an interest in knowing God's desire for your life and relationship. And I pray that you will take an honest and soul-searching look at what God has to say about cohabitation, and seriously reconsider your present views or living arrangements.

God does not take cohabitation lightly, and you shouldn't either. Here are a few questions that I hope you'll consider.

Why is cohabitation any different than marriage?

Isn't marriage just a piece of paper? If we love each other, and are faithful to the relationship, aren't we considered married in God's eyes? Why is our relationship any different than a marriage?

These are the kinds of questions that many cohabitating couples have, and they are sincere questions. If marriage is about love and commitment, why do you need a license and a ceremony? Doesn't God recognize our commitment the same way he does a marriage?

This may sound like a good argument, but the reality is, cohabitation is the exact opposite of commitment. That's why it is not recognized as a legal marriage—by the government, the church, or by God. The intent of living together is to avoid the commitment of marriage. When you are living together, you can leave at any time without consequence. So can your partner. You are not bound by law, nor any other entity. And in God's eyes, you are not married, no matter how committed or loving you feel—because you haven't entered into the covenant of marriage.

Your relationship is a living arrangement, not a covenant. And there is a big difference.

Why is covenant so important?

God is a covenantal God. Covenant is how he chooses to communicate with us. He redeemed us through covenant, and guaranteed us eternal life through the covenantal blood of Jesus. The Bible is a covenantal document, made up of the Old and New Testaments. And the word "testament" in Latin is "Covenant." The word covenant means "to cut." You don't make a covenant; you "cut covenant."

"EVERY EARTHLY RELATIONSHIP YOU ENTER INTO WILL EITHER BE BASED ON FEAR, OR ON FAITH. AND YOU HAVE TO CHOOSE WHICH OPTION YOU WILL TAKE."

The first marriage between Adam and Eve was described in the second chapter of Genesis when God "cut" Adam and took a rib from his side to create his wife, Eve. The New Covenant of salvation came when Jesus was crucified on the cross and he bled to pay for our sins.

In relationships, you get what you pay for. Moving your clothes into someone else's closet isn't a commitment; it's a living arrangement. And if that's what you do, it is all you will ever get out of the relationship. It is cheap and easy.

But covenant is the exact opposite. The word covenant implies a sacrificial, permanent relationship. It begins with a solemn oath of loyalty, where couples commit to staying true to each other "for better or worse, in sickness and in health, for richer and for poorer, until death does them part." These are covenantal vows.

In today's society, many couples recite these vows without really understanding them. But marriage only works when it is a covenantal relationship between two people. You may have had sexual relations in the past, or lived with someone because you didn't understand this truth. God is a graceful God, and he will forgive you of your past, but he expects you to do your part and begin seeing marriage as a sacred covenant that requires sacrifice and commitment.

God deals with man through covenant, because covenant is the language of God's heart. He brings us into relationship with himself through covenant, and he binds our hearts together in marriage through covenant with each other.

A wedding is a covenantal ceremony. It is our way of acknowledging our commitment to both God and society, and of binding ourselves to each other, legally, spiritually, and physically. It is far more than a piece of paper.

There is no room in God's paradigm for "shacking up," or living together, or "cohabitating." These things are a direct affront to God, because they all shake their fist at covenant. Sex before marriage is wrong because it is sex without the blessing and commitment of covenant.

In God's economy, without covenant there is no relationship, only a pattern of willful disobedience and sin.

I'm living with my partner and I'd like to get married, but we can't afford to live apart. Can't we just stay together and plan to get married?

A lot of couples have found themselves in this exact situation, and it feels like the compassionate answer would be to say, "Just stay together and try not to have sexual relations until you have the money to get married." But that is not only bad advice; it's patently unrealistic.

In every situation I've seen, couples are cohabitating so that they don't have to get married. Men usually want to live together because they are afraid of commitment, and they want to try out the relationship to see if it works. Women usually agree to live with men because they are eager to take the relationship to the next level. Marriage is more often a sticking point in the relationship, not something they are "saving up" to do.

Also, assuming that couples who live together will have the discipline to abstain from sex until they are married is always a bad assumption. It was a desire for sex that brought them together, and the temptation will only grow greater if they try to stay apart while under the same roof.

The only loving answer to this question is, "If you want God to bless your relationship, you begin by separating and abstaining from sex until you get married." If you can't afford it, you may have to move in with a friend or sibling, or back home with your parents. There is always a way to make it work if you are committed to following God's will for your relationship.

What if I move out and lose my partner over it?

If you move out and your partner leaves, that tells you everything you need to know about their level of commitment to both you and your relationship. If their only interest in you was as a live-in companion, then marriage was never going to be in your future. It may be a hard truth to learn, but one you need to know now, before wasting another minute on a dead-end relationship.

Every earthly relationship you enter into will either be based on fear, or on faith. And you have to choose which option you will take.

A relationship based on fear says, If I don't hang onto this person, no one else will come along. I don't want to lose them. I know that living together is wrong, but my circumstance is different than others. I've never had anyone, and I may never find another partner. I can't let them get away!

Fear is the devil's favorite playground, and he loves dragging us there with him. But no decision based on fear is ever the right choice.

The right choice is faith, and a relationship based on faith says, If I do the right thing, God's blessing will follow. If our relationship is of God, he will keep us together. If it isn't, he will bless me with a relationship that is.

Faith is believing that God is always in control. And that he always has your best interest in mind, even when things don't work out as you might expect.

What if we get married and the marriage doesn't work out?

This is really the question that is at the heart of the cohabitation movement. When the rate of divorce started going up, many young people took notice, and they began losing faith in the reliability of marriage. At the root of most cohabitating relationships is a small inner-voice saying, "We don't know if this is going to work, so let's try each other out before we commit."

It's a good question to ask, and it's an even better one for us to end this book on, because it's something every couple contemplating marriage is wondering—

maybe not openly, but somewhere deep in their spirit.

How do we know we can make this marriage work?

The reality is, marriage is likely to be one of the biggest challenges you will ever face, and it's normal to worry about whether you are capable of going the distance. It takes more than a desire to be together to keep your relationship from imploding. And the first few years of your marriage will test your relationship in ways you never dreamed possible.

There is a truth about marriage that you may have never heard from your parents, or your married friends, or even your pastor, though it's something every couple considering marriage needs to hear. So let's not gloss over it.

When you are married, there will be times when you feel like calling it quits. There will be days when you are tempted to throw up your hands in frustration and give in. There will be nights when you go to bed thoroughly convinced that you've married the wrong person, and then wake up in the morning feeling even more discouraged and confused. There will be arguments that seem to go on forever, disagreements that will feel like deal-breakers, annoying habits that will seem unbearable, and disputes that can easily lead to your undoing if you let them.

There will be days when the devil is determined to get his way. And on those days, he will be relentless in trying to rip your marriage apart.

On those days, there is only one thing that will keep you from throwing in the towel and giving up. And that is a shared covenantal commitment to both God and to each other that is grounded in faith, and wholly non-negotiable.

If you don't have that sense of commitment, your marriage is very likely to fail. If you don't have a covenantal paradigm that runs to the core of your being, you may not make it. If divorce is an option in the back of your mind, you might as well start looking for lawyers.

Satan hates marriage with every fiber of his being, and he can sense a waning resolve from across the planet. If you want your marriage to last, you have to go into it with a level of commitment that is unmistakable and undeterred. You have to have a faith that says, "No matter how hard this gets, we will not give in. No matter how great our disagreements, we will work them out. No matter how tempted we are to quit, we will make this marriage work!"

You have to know in your heart that God will bring you through any hardship and trial the devil throws your way, if you just stay the course, and remain in God's will.

The blessings of a covenantal marriage are both immense and eternal. There is nothing on earth more intimately rewarding and satisfying than a truly great marriage. And with the right attitude, it's a blessing that any couple can experience first hand!

That is our final hope and prayer for you.

Don't miss out on God's greatest blessing for your future. Find the right one for you, and then seal your commitment in a covenantal marriage relationship. Then watch the floodgates of blessing open wide!

Finding

The

Right One

An Interactive Workbook
for Individuals or Groups

Rock Solid
PARTNERS

It's not often you get the opportunity to make your own life better while helping thousands of others at the same time. But you can do that right now by saying "yes" to becoming a Rock Solid Partner.

MarriageToday has spent years developing proven tools for healing the most shattered of relationships and for making good marriages truly great. When you say "yes" to joining the ranks of MarriageToday's Rock Solid Partners, you get the good feeling that comes from knowing you are having a powerful, positive impact on the lives of children and their parents.

You also get exclusive access to our monthly *Dream Marriage Library* resource – a bundle of topical help and insight that is already transforming relationships all over America and around the world.

MONTHLY DONATION OPTIONS

$**14**
month

DIGITAL LIBRARY ACCESS

$**28**
month

+ MONTHLY DVD'S IN THE MAIL

$**56**
month

+ PARTNER PERKS

Sign up now by visiting
MARRIAGETODAY.COM/PARTNERS

Happy, Happy Love

Tips & Techniques to Refresh Your Marriage
and Restore the Romance

Refresh your romance with *Happy, Happy
Love*, a new book from MarriageToday!
Designed to recharge your marriage, it's
bursting with a delightful blend of suggestions
and inspiration.

$14.95

To order visit www.marriagetoday.com

Marriage on the Rock

From communication to money to sex, Marriage on the Rock is the best-selling book that clearly deals with all the major issues a couple will encounter. Leading marriage authority Jimmy Evans discusses practical real-life challenges and offers easy to understand solutions even if you are the only one willing to work on the relationship.

BK01.........Paperback Book
CD011.......5-CD Series
DVD001...3-DVD Series
CK011.......Curriculum Kit

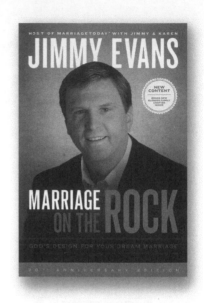

Freedom From Your Past

The past isn't really the past until it has been reconciled in Christ. Without properly addressing the pain and problems of the past, your present and future are adversely affected. In fact, many problems in relationships, emotions and attitudes are linked to unresolved issues. But here's the good news! You can find *Freedom From Your Past* by understanding and dealing with these issues in a biblical manner. You can put your past to rest. You can begin living the life of freedom God has designed for you!

BK05.......Book

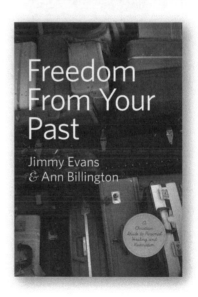

To order call 1-800-380-6330
or visit www.marriagetoday.com

MARRIAGETODAY

CONTACT INFORMATION

P.O. Box 59888
Dallas, TX 75229
972-953-0500

www.marriagetoday.com